Education Language Arts

MW01691098

Grade 5: Module 2

Student Workbook

EL Education Language Arts Curriculum

Grade 5: Language Arts: Module 2: Biodiversity in the Rainforest, Student Workbook (Second Edition)

EL Education Language Arts Curriculum is published by:

EL Education

247 W. 35th Street, 8th Floor

New York, NY 10001

www.ELeducation.org

ISBN 978-1683623328

SECOND EDITION

Cover art from "Birds of the Palouse," a project by first and second grade students at Palouse Prairie Charter School in Moscow, Idaho. For more information about this project, visit <http://modelsofexcellence.ELeducation.org/projects/birds-palouse>.

5 6 7 8 9 10 1.1

About EL Education

"There is more in us than we know. If we can be made to see it, perhaps, for the rest of our lives, we will be unwilling to settle for less." – Kurt Hahn

EL Education (formerly Expeditionary Learning) is redefining student achievement in diverse communities across the country, ensuring that all students master rigorous content, develop positive character, and produce high-quality work. We create great public schools where they are needed most, inspiring teachers and students to achieve more than they thought possible.

EL Education's portfolio of instructional materials and coaching services draws on 25 years of success in more than 150 schools in the EL Education network, serving over 4,000 teachers and 50,000 students in 30 states. Based on our founding principles of meaningful work, character, and respect for teachers, EL Education's offerings transform teaching and learning to promote habits of scholarship and character that lead to high student achievement, regardless of student background. In addition to success on standardized tests, EL Education students demonstrate critical thinking, intellectual courage, and emotional resilience; they possess the passion and the capacity to contribute to a better world.

EL Education's curriculum is a comprehensive, standards-based core literacy program that engages teachers and students through compelling, real world content. Our Language Arts curriculum is used across the country, and has been downloaded more than 8 million times. The curriculum has received the highest marks from EdReports.org and Educators Evaluating the Quality of Instructional Products (EQuIP).

For more information, visit www.ELeducation.org.

Grade 5: Module 2

Unit 1

Problem and Solution Structure: *The Most Beautiful Roof in the World*, Pages 9–10 Graphic Organizer

RI.5.5

Name: ______________________ **Date:** ______________

***How does the way a text is structured support our understanding of complex ideas?**

Text:

PROBLEM

↓ ↓

SOLUTION
Evidence that explains at least two ways scientists overcame the problem:

Summary: *The Most Beautiful Roof in the World*, Pages 9–10

RI.5.2

On pages 9–10 of *The Most Beautiful Roof in the World*, Kathryn Lasky explains that the rainforest canopy is difficult to study. It is very high up, making the climb hard for scientists. Other natural obstacles, such as stinging ants, rotten tree trunks, and thorns, make the climb dangerous and difficult. However, new technology and smart, skillful scientists have found ways to study the canopy. New technology has helped scientists overcome the natural obstacles, and scientists are stronger and more fearless than ever. They are like pioneers exploring an undiscovered continent.

Finding the Gist and Unfamiliar Vocabulary: *The Most Beautiful Roof in the World:* "Out of the Shadow and into the Light"

RI.5.4, L.5.4

Name: ______________________________ **Date:** ______________

Text	**Gist** What is it mostly about?	**Unfamiliar Vocabulary**	**Meaning** (use a dictionary if you need to)
Page 12 Beginning with "Deep in Belize ..."			
Page 13 Beginning with "Meg Lowman believes ..."			
Page 14 Beginning with "Meg is up ..."			

Text	Gist What is it mostly about?	Unfamiliar Vocabulary	Meaning (use a dictionary if you need to)
Page 15 Beginning with "The boys have ..."			
Page 16 Beginning with "... hundred feet (thirty meters) ..."			
Page 17 Beginning with "Meg has now ..."			
Pages 19–20 Beginning with "Leaf number five ..."			
Page 22 Beginning with "Meg climbs higher ..."			

Text	Gist What is it mostly about?	Unfamiliar Vocabulary	Meaning (use a dictionary if you need to)
Page 23 Beginning with "Meg clips her ..."			
Page 24 Beginning with "There are many such ..."			
Pages 25–26 Beginning with "Meg carefully edges ..."			

Close Read: *The Most Beautiful Roof in the World*, Pages 11–12 Note-catcher

RI.5.1, RI.5.2, RI.5.4, RI.5.5, L.5.4, L.5.4a, L.5.4b, L.5.4c

Name: ______________________ **Date:** ______________

In this shadowed world, pierced occasionally by slivers of sunlight, are more varieties of living things than perhaps any other place on earth.

Sketch what the rainforest is like. Label your sketch with words and phrases from the text that help you understand what the rainforest is like. **(RI.5.1)**

Descriptive Structure: *The Most Beautiful Roof in the World,* Pages 11–12 Graphic Organizer

RI.5.5

Name: ______________________________ **Date:** ______________

***How does the way a text is structured support our understanding of complex ideas?**

Text: ______________________________

Finding the Gist and Unfamiliar Vocabulary: "Rainforests and Why They Are Important"

RI.5.4, L.5.4

Name: ____________________ **Date:** ____________

Text	Gist What is it mostly about?	Unfamiliar Vocabulary	Meaning (use a dictionary if you need to)
biological diversity			
cultural diversity			
climate stability			

Text Structure Resource Page

RI.5.5

Structure	Description	Graphic Organizer
Problem and Solution	The author gives evidence of a problem and one or more ways to solve it.	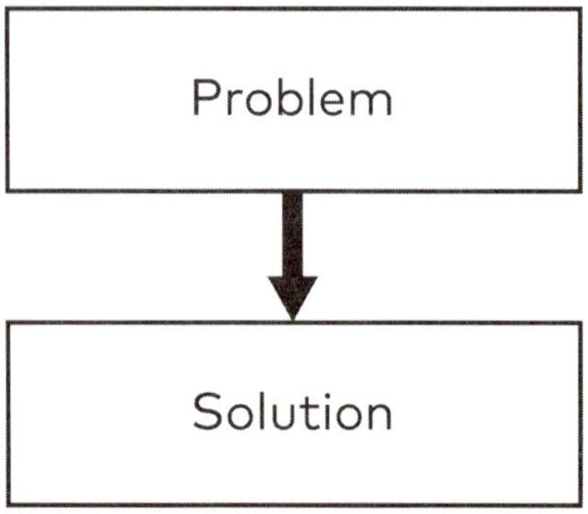
Descriptive	The author tells the characteristics of a topic.	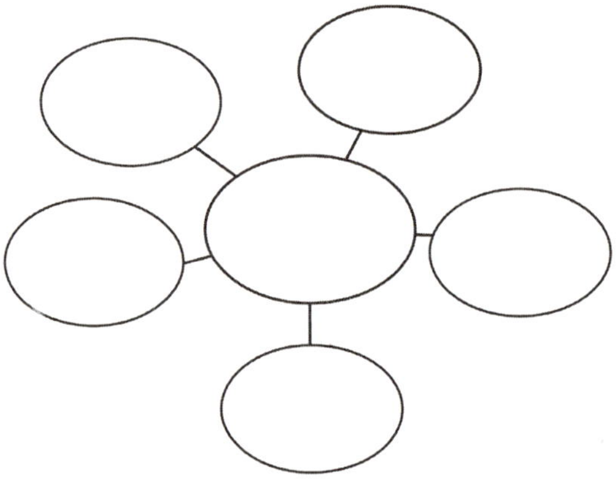
Proposition and Support	The author states a main idea or claim and gives details or evidence to support that idea or claim.	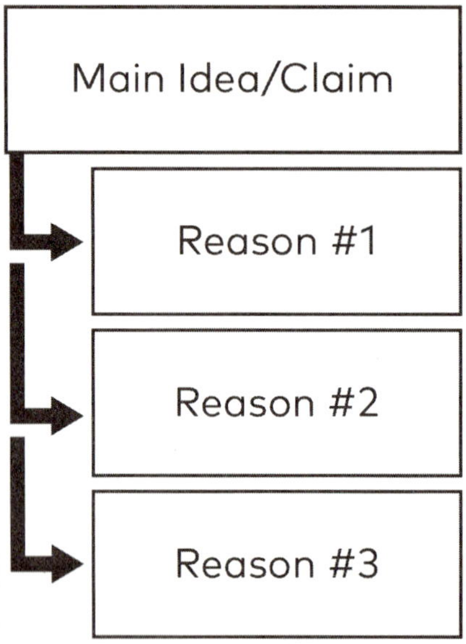

Structure	Description	Graphic Organizer
Chronological/ Sequential	The author relates a sequence of events or steps in a process.	1. _____ First,__________ 2. _____ Second,________ 3. _____ Third, __________ 4. _____ Next, ___________ 5. _____ Finally,__________
Cause and Effect	The author explains the reason something is happening and what happened as a result.	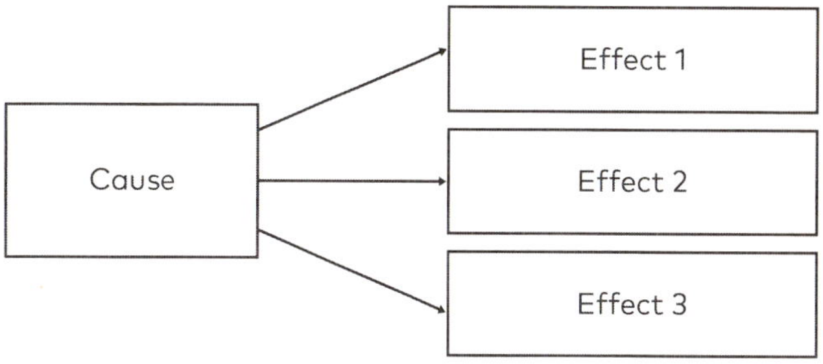
Comparison	The author explains how two things or ideas are the same/ different.	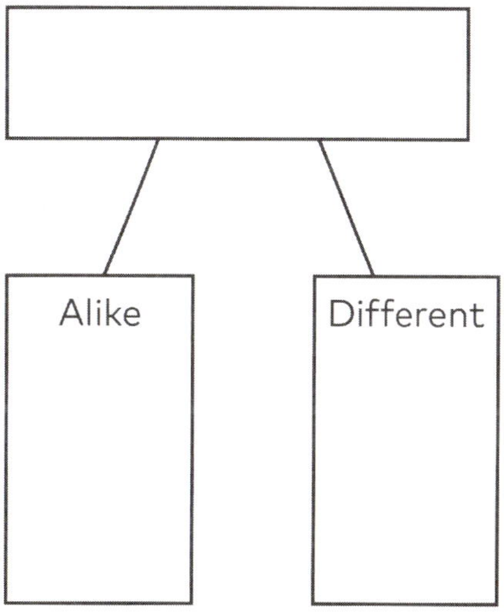

Proposition and Support Structure: "Rainforests and Why They Are Important" Graphic Organizer

RI.5.5

Name: ______________________________ **Date:** ______________

***How does the way a text is structured support our understanding of complex ideas?**

Text:

MAIN IDEA/CLAIM	
	REASON #1 Evidence that the rainforest is important:
	REASON #2 Evidence that the rainforest is important:
	REASON #3 Evidence that the rainforest is important:

Comparing Text Structures I Graphic Organizer

RI.5.5

Name: ________________________________ **Date:** ______________

Directions: *Refer to the texts and your graphic organizers to complete the Venn diagram below.*

- How is the information given in the two texts different? How is it the same?

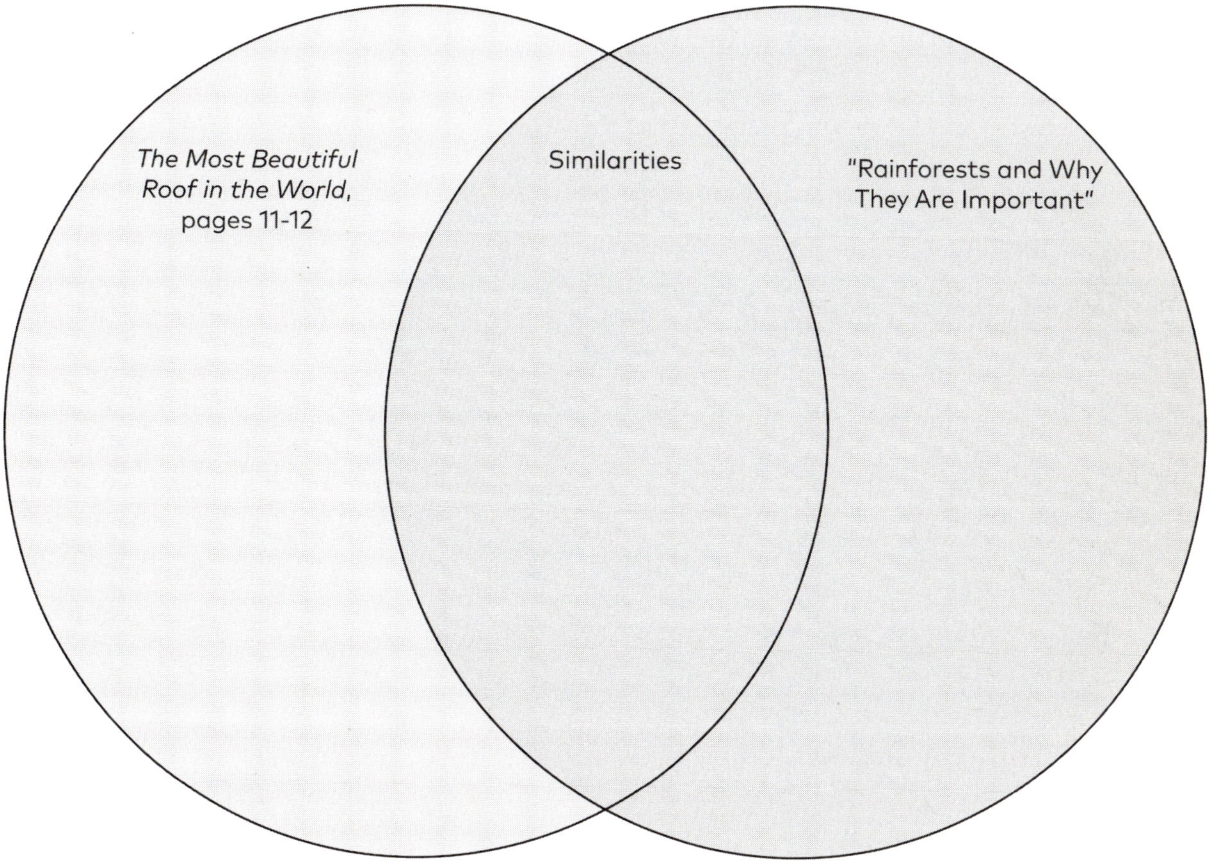

Research: "Rainforests and Why They Are Important" Note-catcher

RI.5.7, W.5.7, W.5.8

Name: ______________________________ **Date:** ______________

Question: Why do scientists study the rainforest?

Source (Author. Web page title. Web page link. Date accessed):	
When I read or see that (evidence) …	**It makes me think that scientists study the rainforest because …**
(Example) "Tropical rainforests are thought to contain around 50% of all the Earth's species of plants and animals."	(Example) There are a lot of different species for them to find out more about.

When I read or see that (evidence) ...	It makes me think that scientists study the rainforest because ...

Close Read: *The Most Beautiful Roof in the World*, Pages 17–20 Note-catcher

RI.5.1, RI.5.2, RI.5.4, RI.5.5, L.5.4

Name: ______________________ **Date:** ____________

Use information from pages 17–20 of *The Most Beautiful Roof in the World* to sketch what Meg is doing. Write a caption with words and phrases from the text.

Language Dive Note-catcher: *The Most Beautiful Roof in the World*

Name: ______________________ **Date:** ______________

The space between the branches changes with each new grip, making a shifting geometry against the sky of sliding rectangles, split-second parabolas, and drifting squares.

Sketch a **parabola.**	Sketch the branches of a **tree**. Circle **the space between the branches.**

Sketch **a shifting geometry against the sky of rectangles, parabolas, and squares.**
Complete the cause and effect sentence to talk about the rainforest or your own life.
The ______________ changes, making ______________. (cause) (effect)

Chronological Structure: *The Most Beautiful Roof in the World*, Pages 17–20 Graphic Organizer

RI.5.5

Name: ______________________________ **Date:** ______________

***How does the way a text is structured support our understanding of complex ideas?**

Text:

List three to five events that explain what Meg does in the canopy, in the order in which they occurred:

1st event	
2nd event	
3rd event	
4th event	
5th event	

Exit Ticket: Comparing Text Structures

RI.5.5

Name: ______________________________ **Date:** ______________

Directions: *Answer the question below.*

Part A

Which sentence **best** states a difference between how information is presented on page 12 of *The Most Beautiful Roof in the World* and how information is presented on pages 17–20 of *The Most Beautiful Roof in the World?*

A. Page 12 of *The Most Beautiful Roof in the World* puts the reader in the role of a rainforest scientist, and pages 17–20 describe plants and animals in the rainforest.

B. Page 12 of *The Most Beautiful Roof in the World* describes a rainforest, and pages 17–20 explain what one scientist does as she studies the rainforest.

C. Page 12 of *The Most Beautiful Roof in the World* focuses on the emotional effects of exploring the rainforest canopy, and pages 17–20 share statistics to provide more information about rainforests.

D. Page 12 of *The Most Beautiful Roof in the World* offers details about the experience of a rainforest scientist, and pages 17–20 discuss the reasons scientists study the rainforest.

Part B

Write **two** details from the texts that support the answer to Part A. Write one detail from page 12 of *The Most Beautiful Roof in the World* and one detail from pages 17–20 of *The Most Beautiful Roof in the World.*

____

____

____

____

____

"Effects of Studying Rainforests"

Scientists have been studying the rainforest for many years. The rainforest abounds with mysteries about the plants and animals that live there, and new species are being discovered every day. Through careful observation of plant life, the climate, and animals that live there, scientists learn more about the rainforest. But what are the effects of studying the rainforest?

Discovery of New Plants and Animals

One effect of studying the rainforest is the discovery of new plants and animals. For thousands of years, people have used plants and animals from the rainforest for farming, clothing, and medicine. More recently, the National Cancer Institute has estimated that about 70 percent of known anti-cancer plants come from the rainforest, and scientists continue to discover new species of plants and animals. Between 1999 and 2009, over 1,200 plants and animals were discovered in the Amazon. That's one new species every three days! As new species continue to come to light, the potential for new, life-saving medicines developed from rainforest plants grows.

Learning about Climate Stability

Another effect of studying the rainforest is developing a better understanding of how rainforests impact the world's climate. Rainforests are known as the "lungs of the planet" because of their role in absorbing carbon dioxide and producing oxygen. Scientists are still learning how rainforests give back to the ecosystem—how they regulate temperature and weather patterns and how they affect the water cycle. Understanding how rainforests impact Earth's climate helps scientists learn how to prepare for climate change. For example, scientists are now working with farmers in South America to rebuild the rainforest through reforestation, or planting new trees, and preserving forests.

Developing New Theories about the Rainforest

Studying the rainforest also helps scientists to develop new theories about the plants and animals that live there. A new theory suggests that in addition to being the "lungs of the planet," the rainforest can also be thought of as a pump, like a heart. Some scientists think the rainforest pumps water through the ecosystem, which might explain why the Amazon has survived for so long.

Curiosity drives scientists' work, and they are always striving to learn more about what they are studying. Because of the importance of rainforests, rainforest scientists' studies affect all of us.

1100L
Written by EL Education for instructional purposes

Sources:

"About the Amazon." *WWF*. World Wildlife Fund, n.d. Web. 19 Jan. 2016. <http://wwf.panda.org/what_we_do/where_we_work/amazon/about_the_amazon/>.

"Climate Change in the Amazon." *WWF*. World Wildlife Fund, n.d. Web. 19 Jan. 2016. <http://www.worldwildlife.org/pages/climate-change-in-the-amazon>.

"8 Easy Ways to Green Your Home." *Rainforest Alliance*. Rainforest Alliance, n.d. Web. 19 Jan. 2016. <https://www.rainforest-alliance.org/articles/green-your-home>.

"Rain Forest: Incubators of Life." *National Geographic*. National Geographic Society, n.d. Web. 19 Jan. 2016. <http://environment.nationalgeographic.com/environment/habitats/rainforest-profile/>.

"Scientists Say the Amazon Is Still Teaching Us New Lessons." NPR. National Public Radio, 6 Dec. 2015. Web. 19 Jan. 2016. <http://www.npr.org/templates/transcript/transcript.php?storyId=454736397>.

Butler, Rhett. "Why Are Rainforests Important?" *Kids.Mongabay.com*. Mongabay.com, 5 Dec. 2015. Web. 19 Jan. 2016. <http://kids.mongabay.com/elementary/401.html>.

"Why Is the Amazon Rainforest Important?" *WWF*. World Wildlife Fund, n.d. Web. 19 Jan. 2016. <http://wwf.panda.org/what_we_do/where_we_work/amazon/about_the_amazon/why_amazon_important/>.

Finding the Gist and Unfamiliar Vocabulary: "Effects of Studying Rainforests"

RI.5.4, L.5.4

Name: ______________________ **Date:** __________

Text	**Gist** What is it mostly about?	**Unfamiliar Vocabulary**	**Meaning** (use a dictionary if you need to)
Introduction			
Discovery of New Plants and Animals			
Learning about Climate Stability			
Developing New Theories about the Rainforest			

Cause and Effect Structure: "Effects of Studying Rainforests" Graphic Organizer

RI.5.5

Name: ______________________________ **Date:** ________________

***How does the way a text is structured support our understanding of complex ideas?**

Text: ______________________________

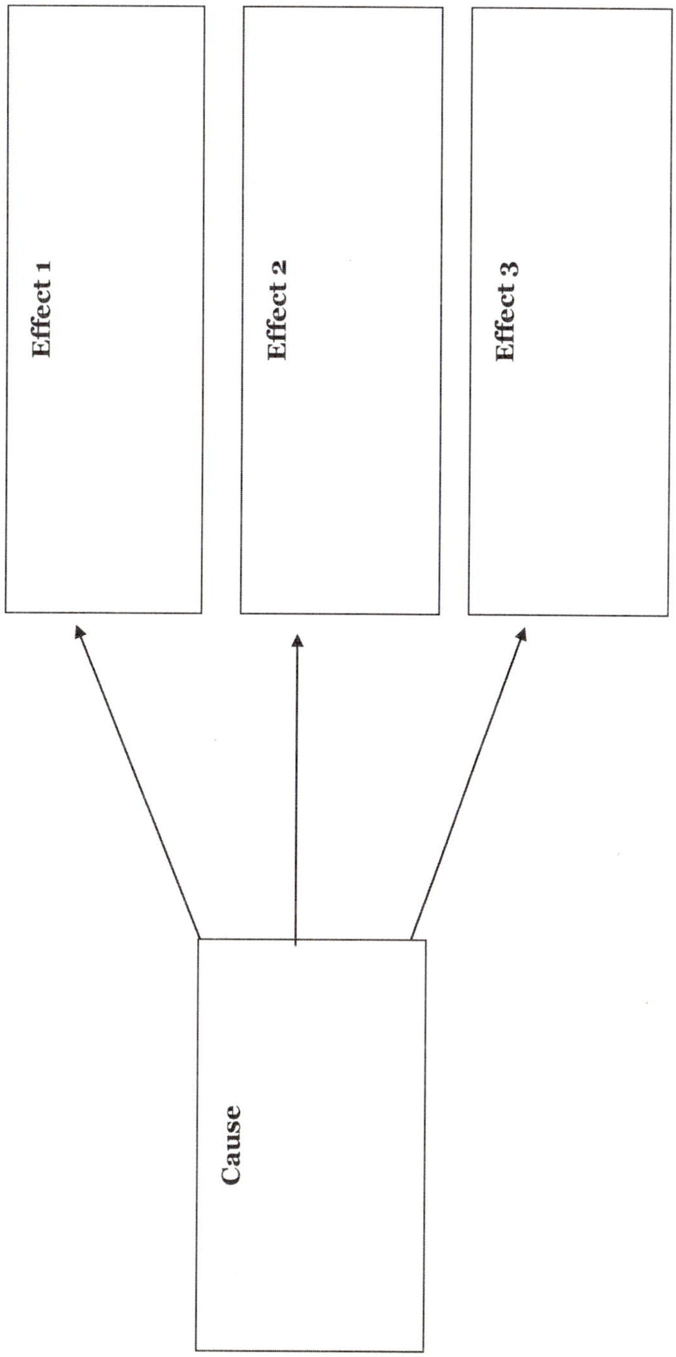

Comparing Text Structures II Graphic Organizer

RI.5.5

Name: ______________________ **Date:** ______________

Directions: *Refer to the texts and your graphic organizers to complete the Venn diagram below.*

- **How is the information given in the two texts different? How is it the same?**

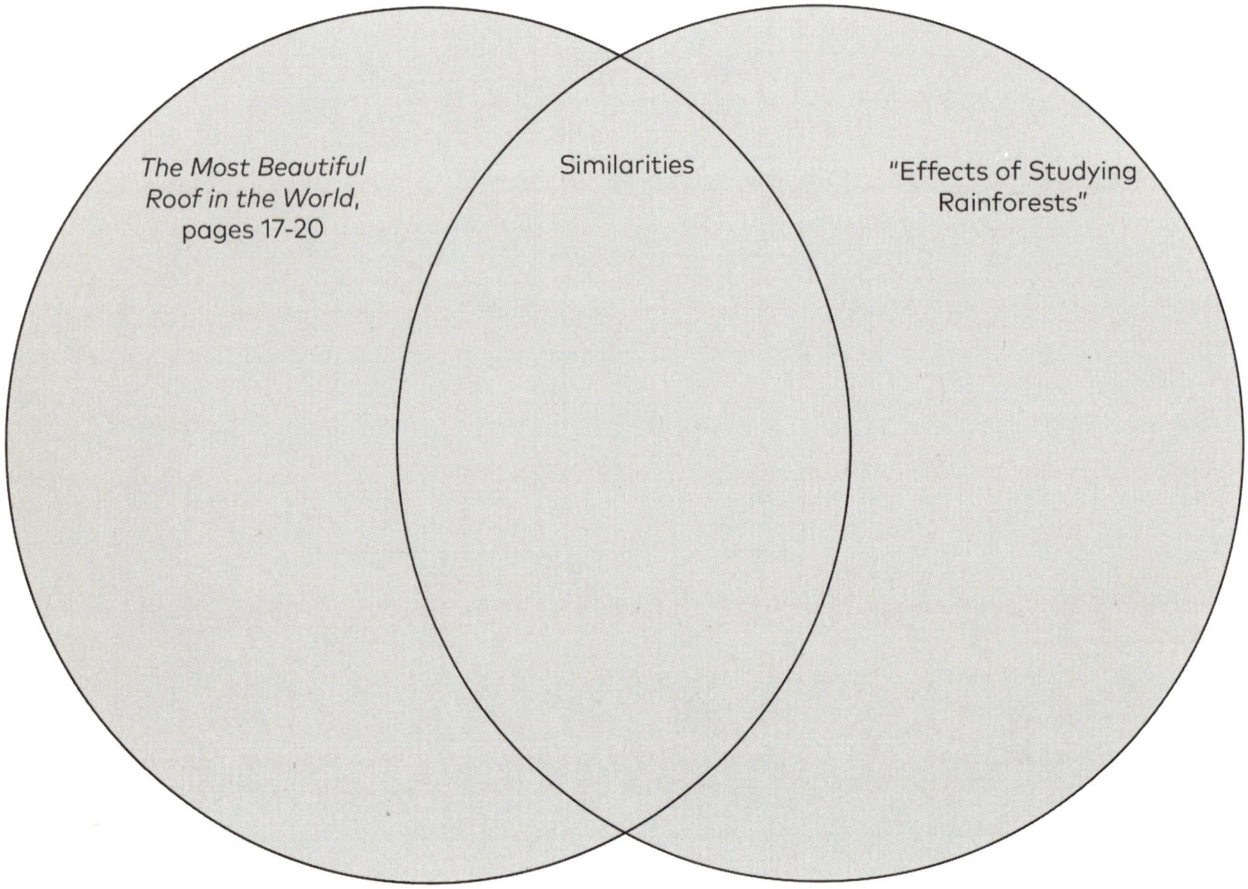

Tracking Progress: Reading, Understanding, and Explaining New Text

Name: ______________________ **Date:** ____________

Learning Target: I can independently read, understand, and explain the meaning of a new text.

Standards I'm Tracking: RL/RI.5.1, RL.5.4, RL.5.10, L.5.4

Text Type (circle): Informative Story Poem Play/Readers Theater

1. How am I doing?

- For each criterion, self-assess by putting a check mark in the appropriate column.
- Write the number of each standard on a sticky note or flag. Then, on your assessment materials, place each sticky note in an area that shows evidence you have met the criteria. This might be next to a selected response question or a short piece of writing. Make sure you have evidence for each criterion.
- Strive to be honest with yourself. Remember, your ability grows with your effort, so it's fine if you aren't there yet!

You will receive feedback on different colored sticky notes/flags and in a different colored pen on the checklist.

Reading, Understanding, and Explaining a New Text					
Standard	**Criteria for reading, understanding, and explaining a new text**	**4 On target**	**3 Getting there**	**2 Working on it**	**1 Need support**
RL.5.1/ RI.5.1	I can quote accurately to explain what a text says and to make inferences.				

Reading, Understanding, and Explaining a New Text					
Standard	**Criteria for reading, understanding, and explaining a new text**	**4 On target**	**3 Getting there**	**2 Working on it**	**1 Need support**
RL.4.4/ RI.4.4 **L.4.4**	I can determine the meaning of unknown words and phrases, including figurative language, using at least one of the following strategies: • Use context. • Use affixes and roots. • Use reference materials.				
RL.5.10/ RI.5.10	I can read and understand grade 5-level texts independently.				

2. How have I improved since I last worked on this skill?

____

____

____

Teacher Response:

____

____

____

3. How can I improve next time?

___

___

___

Teacher Response:

___

___

___

Anchor Standards:

R.1
By the end of Grade 12, I will be able to: Read closely to determine what the text says explicitly and to make logical inferences from it; cite specific textual evidence when writing or speaking to support conclusions drawn from the text.

R.4
By the end of Grade 12, I will be able to: Interpret words and phrases as they are used in a text, including determining technical, connotative, and figurative meanings, and analyze how specific word choices shape meaning or tone.

R.10
By the end of Grade 12, I will be able to: Read and comprehend complex literary and informational texts independently and proficiently.

L.4
By the end of Grade 12, I will be able to: Determine or clarify the meaning of unknown and multiple-meaning words and phrases by using context clues, analyzing meaningful word parts, and consulting general and specialized reference materials, as appropriate.

Why Scientists Study the Rainforest: Preparing for a Science Talk Note-catcher

SL.5.1

Name: ______________________ **Date:** ____________

Question: Why do scientists study the rainforest?

Preparation: Look back in your texts about the rainforest to find evidence to help you answer the Science Talk question.

When I read or see that (evidence) ...	It makes me think that scientists study the rainforest because ...
(Example) "In this shadowed world, pierced occasionally by slivers of sunlight, are more varieties of living things than perhaps any other place on earth." (*The Most Beautiful Roof in the World*, page 11)	(Example) There are a lot of different species for them to find out more about.

Science Talk Notes and Goals

SL.5.1c, SL.5.1d

Name: ______________________________ **Date:** ______________

My Science Talk Notes: Ideas and Questions
Key Ideas:

My Conclusions:

My goals for the Next Science Talk:
My Teacher's Feedback:

Helping the Rainforest Links

RI.5.7, W.5.7, W.5.8

Source 1	Rainforest Foundation	https://dev.rainforestfoundation.org/wp-content/uploads/2015/10/Things-You-Should-Know.pdf
Source 2	Conserve Energy Future	https://www.conserve-energy-future.com/surprising-and-innovative-ways-for-you-to-save-rainforests.php
Source 3	Adventure Life	http://www.adventure-life.com/amazon/articles/what-can-i-do

What Can I Do to Help the Rainforest? Note-catcher

RI.5.7, W.5.7, W.5.8

Name: ______________________ **Date:** ____________

Source 1	
Source (Author. Web page title. Web page link. Date accessed):	
Summary:	
When I read or see that (evidence) ...	**It makes me think that to help save the rainforest, I can ...**

Source 2	
Source (Author. Web page title. Web page link. Date accessed):	
Summary:	
When I read or see that (evidence) ...	**It makes me think that to help save the rainforest, I can ...**

Source 3	
Source (Author. Web page title. Web page link. Date accessed):	
Summary:	
When I read or see that (evidence) ...	**It makes me think that to help save the rainforest, I can ...**

Exit Ticket: What Can I Do to Help the Rainforest?

Name: ______________________ **Date:** ____________

From your research today, what is one way you found you can help the rainforest? How does it help the rainforest?

____

____

____

____

____

Tracking Progress: Research

Name: ______________________ **Date:** ______________

Learning Target: I can gather information through research to build knowledge and answer research questions.

Standards I'm Tracking: W.5.7 and **W.5.8**

Text Type (circle): Informative Story Poem Play/Readers Theater

1. How am I doing?

- For each criterion, self-assess by putting a check mark in the appropriate column.
- Write the number of each standard on a sticky note or flag. Then on your own writing, place each sticky note in an area that shows evidence you have met that criterion. Make sure you have evidence for each criterion.
- Strive to be honest with yourself. Remember, your ability grows with your effort, so it's fine if you aren't there yet!

You will receive feedback on different colored sticky notes/flags and in a different colored pen on the checklist.

Standard	Characteristics of Effective Research	4 Advanced	3 Proficient	2 Developing	1 Beginning
W.5.7	I can investigate different aspects of a topic to build knowledge and/or answer research questions.				
W.5.8	I can take notes and categorize information from several print and digital sources.				

Standard	Characteristics of Effective Research	4 Advanced	3 Proficient	2 Developing	1 Beginning
W.5.8	I can summarize or paraphrase information collected in research in notes and finished work.				
W.5.8	I can list my sources.				

2. How have I improved since I last worked on this skill?

____

____

____

Teacher Response:

____

____

____

3. How can I improve next time?

____

____

____

Teacher Response:

____

____

____

Anchor Standards:

W.7
By the end of Grade 12 I will be able to: Conduct short as well as more sustained research projects based on focused questions, demonstrating understanding of the subject under investigation.

W.8
By the end of Grade 12 I will be able to: Gather relevant information from multiple print and digital sources, assess the credibility and accuracy of each source, and integrate the information while avoiding plagiarism.

Notices and Wonders Note-catcher

Name: ______________________ **Date:** ______________

Resource	I Notice	I Wonder
1		
2		
3		
4		

Tracking Progress: Collaborative Discussion

Name: ______________________________ **Date:** ______________

Learning Target: I can participate in an effective collaborative discussion.

Standards I'm Tracking: SL.5.1

1. How am I doing?

- For each criterion, self-assess by putting a check mark in the appropriate column.
- Strive to be honest with yourself. Remember, your ability grows with your effort, so it's fine if you aren't there yet!

You will receive feedback in a different colored pen on the checklist.

Standard	Characteristics of an Effective Collaborative Discussion	4 Advanced	3 Proficient	2 Developing	1 Beginning
SL.5.1a	I prepare for the discussion by finding appropriate evidence in the text(s).				
SL.5.1a	I use the evidence I prepare to support my ideas during the discussion.				
SL.5.1b	I follow agreed-upon rules for the discussion.				
SL.5.1b	I carry out the role I have been given in a discussion.				
***SL.5.1c**	I ask questions to better understand what others are saying.				
***SL.5.1c**	I answer questions to help others understand my ideas.				

Standard	Characteristics of an Effective Collaborative Discussion	4 Advanced	3 Proficient	2 Developing	1 Beginning
***SL.5.1c**	I link my ideas to those of others.				
***SL.5.1c**	I elaborate on others' ideas.				
SL.5.1d	I explain the key ideas of a discussion and how my understanding has grown from it.				

2. How have I improved since I last worked on this skill?

____

____

____

Teacher Response:

____

____

____

3. How can I improve next time?

____

____

____

Teacher Response:

____

____

____

Anchor Standard: SL.1

By the end of Grade 12 I will be able to: Prepare for and participate effectively in a range of conversations and collaborations with diverse partners, building on others' ideas and expressing my own clearly and persuasively.

Grade 5: Module 2: Unit 1

Homework Resources (for Families)

Unit 1: Building Background Knowledge: Why Scientists Study the Rainforest

Common Core State Standards addressed: RI.5.2, RI.5.5, RI.5.7, W.5.7, W.5.8, SL.5.1

Guiding Questions and Big Ideas

Why do scientists study the rainforest?

- *Scientists study the rainforest because it is home to a diversity of life.*
- *Scientists study the rainforest to determine the impact of deforestation on biodiversity.*

What can we do to help the rainforest?

What will your student be doing at school?

In this unit, students build background knowledge about the rainforest, including rainforest destruction, to understand why scientists study the rainforest. In the first half of the unit, they read excerpts of *The Most Beautiful Roof in the World* and other texts to analyze the structure and to summarize the text. For the mid-unit assessment, students read, summarize, and compare the structure of two new informational texts about the rainforest. Having learned about rainforest destruction through texts in the first half of the unit, in the second half of the unit, students do web research to answer the question: "What can I do to help the rainforest?" They prepare for a Science Talk in which they discuss the things they can do to help and also the realistic challenges of implementing some of those things. For the first part of the end of unit assessment, students conduct further research about ways to help the rainforest using new sources. They then use these findings, along with their research from previous lessons, to participate in another Science Talk, which serves as the second part of the end of unit assessment.

Working to contribute to a better world is a habit of character that is emphasized in this unit. These are the specific effective learning skills students will focus on:

- I take care of and improve our shared spaces and the environment.
- I use my strengths to help others grow.
- I apply my learning to help our school, the community, and the environment.

Text Structures

Structure	Description	Graphic Organizer
Descriptive	The author tells the characteristics of a topic.	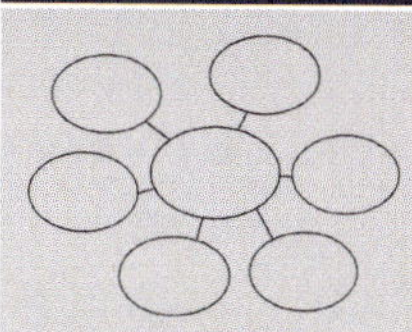
Proposition and Support	The author states a main idea or claim and gives details or evidence to support it.	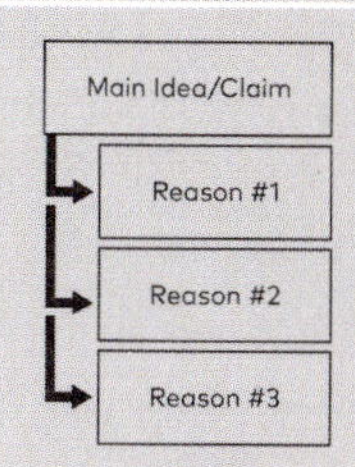
Chronological/ Sequential	The author relates a sequence of events or steps in a process.	1._____ First,___________ 2._____ Second,___________ 3._____ Third, ___________ 4._____ Next, ___________ 5._____ Finally,___________
Cause and Effect	The author explains the reason something is happening and what happened as a result.	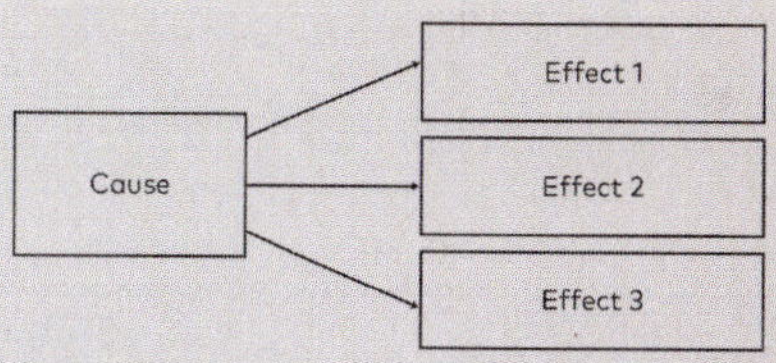
Comparison	The author explains how two things or ideas are the same/ different.	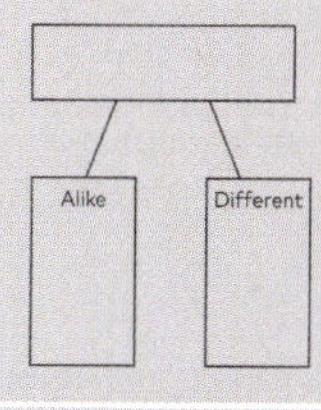
Problem and Solution	The author gives evidence of a problem and one or more ways to solve it.	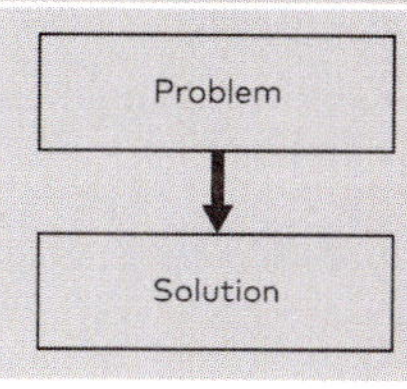

How can you support your student at home?

- Talk to your student about the diversity of life in the rainforest, rainforest destruction, and things he or she can do to help the rainforest.
- Visit local zoos/animal parks and/or botanical gardens to observe rainforest animals and plants.
- Watch documentaries about the rainforest, rainforest animals and plants, and rainforest destruction.
- Work with your student to research rainforests on the internet, specifically the diversity of life, rainforest destruction, and things we can do to help.
- Talk to your student about text structures using the chart above.

- Encourage your student to summarize texts that he or she reads.
- Work with your student to implement some of the things he or she has found to help the rainforest.

Unit 1: Homework

In Lessons 1–8, homework focuses on research reading, summarizing, and vocabulary.

In Lessons 9–13, homework focuses on independent reading and preparing for a collaborative discussion.

Research reading: Your child is expected to independently research the topic by reading topic-related books of his or her choice for approximately 20 minutes **each day** and responding to a prompt of choice in the **front** of the independent reading journal. These are usually books your child will bring home from school; however, they may be topic-related books chosen by the child at the public or home library. Prompts for independent reading can be found in the homework materials provided.

Choice reading: If your child would also like to independently read and respond to a book of free choice, he or she may use the **back** of the independent reading journals. Prompts for independent reading can be found in the homework materials provided.

Lesson	Lesson Content	Homework Practice	Due In	Anticipated Date*
1	Students discover the module topic and are introduced to the final performance task.	1. Research reading and answering prompt	1. Teacher will check independent reading journals strategically.	
2	Students read a new informational text about the rainforest and analyze its structure, read a section from *The Most Beautiful Roof in the World* for the gist, and generate criteria for summaries.	1. Vocabulary 2. Research reading and answering prompt	1. **Lesson 8** 2. Teacher will check independent reading journals strategically.	
3	Students closely read an excerpt from *The Most Beautiful Roof in the World* and read a new text about the rainforest for the gist.	1. Vocabulary 2. For ELLs: Language Dive 1 Practice 3. Research reading and answering prompt	1. **Lesson 8** 2. **Lesson 4** 3. Teacher will check independent reading journals strategically.	
4	Students reread a text about the rainforest to analyze its structure and plan a summary. They use their plan to write a class summary of the text.	1. Summarize a chapter or section of your independent reading book.	1. **Lesson 7**	

*Teacher note: Please complete the 'Anticipated Date' column according to your schedule.

Lesson	Lesson Content	Homework Practice	Due In	Anticipated Date*
5	Students compare the structure of two texts about the rainforest. They reread a text to answer the question: Why do scientists study the rainforest?	1. Vocabulary 2. Research reading and answering prompt	1. **Lesson 8** 2. Teacher will check independent reading journals strategically.	
6	Students closely read an excerpt from *The Most Beautiful Roof in the World*.	1. Summarize a chapter or section of your independent reading book. 2. For ELLs: Language Dive 2 Practice 3. Research reading and answering prompt	1. **Lesson 7** 2. **Lesson 7** 3. Teacher will check independent reading journals strategically.	
7	Students read a new text about the rainforest, analyze its structure, and write a summary. They compare the structure of this text to the excerpt from *The Most Beautiful Roof in the World* read in Lesson 5.	1. Vocabulary 2. Research reading and answering prompt	1. **Lesson 8** 2. Teacher will check independent reading journals strategically.	
8	For the Mid-Unit 1 Assessment, students read and summarize two new texts about the rainforest. Then, they compare the structure of these two texts.	1. Research reading and answering prompt	1. Teacher will check independent reading journals strategically.	
9	Students prepare for a Science Talk in which they will discuss: Why do scientists study the rainforest?	1. Review notes for the Science Talk. 2. Research reading and answering prompt	1. **Lesson 10** 2. Teacher will check independent reading journals strategically.	
10	Students participate in a collaborative discussion about why scientists study the rainforest.	1. Research reading and answering prompt	1. Teacher will check independent reading journals strategically.	
11	Students work in pairs to research online to answer the question: What can I do to help the rainforest?	1. Research reading and answering prompt	1. Teacher will check independent reading journals strategically.	
12	For the End of Unit 1 Assessment, Part I, students research independently to continue to answer the question: What can I do to help the rainforest?	1. Review notes for the Science Talk. 2. Research reading and answering prompt	1. Lesson 13 2. Teacher will check independent reading journals strategically.	
13	For the End of Unit 1 Assessment, Part II, students participate in a collaborative discussion (Science Talk) about things they can do to help the rainforest.	1. Research reading and answering prompt	1. Teacher will check independent reading journals strategically.	

*Teacher note: Please complete the 'Anticipated Date' column according to your schedule.

Independent Reading

Independent Reading Prompts

Directions: Remember to record responses to **research reading in the front** of your independent reading journal and responses to **choice reading in the back**. Try to choose a different prompt each time.

Record any new vocabulary in your vocabulary log. Remember, academic vocabulary is recorded in the front, and domain-specific vocabulary (words about the topic) is recorded in the back. Mark vocabulary found during independent reading with a symbol—an asterisk (*), for example.

Record:

- Date
- Title and author of your reading book
- Pages you have read
- Prompt
- Response

Example:

Date: 04/08/2018

Book Title and Author: *The Most Beautiful Roof in the World* by Kathryn Lasky

Pages Read: 22–27

Prompt: What questions do you have about the rainforest canopy after reading?

Response: What other animals and plants live in the rainforest canopy?

1. **Record two or three facts in your own words about the rainforest or rainforest animals that you found out in your research reading today.**
2. **What questions do you have about the rainforest or rainforest animals after reading?**
3. **What would you like to research further after reading? Why?**
4. **Summarize your research reading today in no more than four sentences.**
5. **How would you describe the setting of the particular part of the text you read?**
   A. Hint: What did you picture in your mind as you were reading it? Why?
   B. Hint: What did it say in the text to make you think that?
6. **What do you think is going to happen next? Why?**
   A. Hint: What has the author written so far to make you think that?
7. **What is the main idea of the part of the text you just read?**
   A. Hint: The main idea is the point the author wants you to understand.

8. **Think about the title of your text. Why do you think the author chose this title?**
   A. Hint: Explain how the title fits the book.
   B. Hint: Start out: "The title of my book is.... The author chose this title because...."
9. **What are two new words you learned in this text? Tell about the words.**
10. **Choose a picture, chart, graph, or diagram from your text. Explain how the information you learned from the image helped you understand the text.**
    A. Hint: First, think about the main idea of what you just read. Then, think about how the picture, chart, graph, or diagram supports the main idea.

Vocabulary

Directions: In the classroom, you have been recording words from your research in your vocabulary log. Throughout this unit, you have been research reading topic-related books at home to build your knowledge of the rainforest, and then recording words in your independent reading journal.

Choose a word or phrase from your research reading or from a text you've read in class and add the word or phrase to your vocabulary log. Try to choose a different word or phrase to add and to practice a different vocabulary strategy each time. For each word, be sure to add the following:

- the definition, or meaning, of the word
- the vocabulary strategy you used to figure out the meaning of the word
- a sketch or diagram that helps you to better understand the meaning of the word

As a reminder, the vocabulary strategies we've been working on in class are:

Vocabulary Strategies

- Context: Read the sentence around the word.
- Look at the affixes for clues.
- Look at the root of the word for clues.
- Use a dictionary.
- Discuss a word with another person (after attempting some of the above strategies).

Homework: Language Dive 1 Practice

Name: ______________________________ **Date:** ______________

1. The sentence below is scrambled. Write it in the correct sequence:

to fill the gaps	It is the very diversity	with a rush of oppor-tunistic species	that allows life to thrive everywhere,	to spring back

____

____

____

____

2. Sketch the meaning of the sentence above.

3. Circle the verbs in the sentence above. What is the author communicating about the rainforest?

The author is communicating _______________________________

____

____.

4. Draw a box around the word that tells what the sentence is mostly about.
5. Underline the words and phrases that are used to talk about connecting things together.
6. Write the sentence above in your own words:

____

____

7. Define the following words:
   1. *Diversity is* ______________________________________.
   2. *To thrive* means ___________________________________.

Homework: Language Dive 2 Practice

Name: ______________________ **Date:** ____________

1. The sentence below is scrambled. Write it in the correct sequence:

changes with each new grip,	making a shifting geometry	The space between the branches	of sliding rectangles, split-second parabolas, and drifting squares	against the sky.

____

____

____

____

2. Sketch the meaning of the sentence above.

3. Sketch a *parabola*:

4. Draw a square around a word that can be a verb or a noun.
5. Write a sentence using the phrase *against the sky*.

6. Circle four words in the sentence that are related to moving.
7. What colors do you imagine as you read this sentence?

Grade 5: Module 2

Unit 2

"The Dreaming Tree"

A Folktale from Brazil

April 24, 2007 | Adapted by Amy Friedman

Once upon a time a young boy named Uaica lived with his grandfather in a small village. He was a kind-hearted child, but he was sickly and tinier than the other boys of his village. He was frequently unwell, and the others teased him and ignored him, so that Uaica was often lonely. His grandfather loved the boy and wanted to protect him from harm, and so did his best to take care of him.

But one day when the boys had been especially cruel, Uaica could not find his grandfather. He walked into the forest, where he always felt happy. The trees offered a beautiful, protective canopy, and exotic flowers spiced the air with fragrant scents. The raucous calls of the macaws and parrots cheered the boy, and when the butterflies softly brushed against his skin, he remembered there was gentleness in this world.

Distracted by the birds and insects around him, he tripped upon a fallen branch, and when he looked down he saw a most amazing sight. There at the foot of an enormous tree lay a tapir, a sloth, an anaconda, a monkey, a caiman and a family of jaguars fast asleep, all curled up beside each other.

Uaica stood and stared in wonder, but as he did, he felt overcome by sleep. "I must not lie down near these wild animals," he said aloud, but he could not help himself. Before he knew what was happening, he was on the ground and fast asleep.

Soon he was dreaming. Someone was whispering in Uaica's ear, "I am Sinaa," the man's voice said, and Uaica knew this was the son of the jaguar. He had heard tales of this Jaguar Man, who had healing powers and eyes in the back of his head. This man was old, but when he bathed, he shed his skin and so he appeared forever young. He knew where the large forked stick that holds up the sky was buried and all the secrets of saving the world.

Sinaa began to tell tales and reveal his secrets to Uaica in his dream.

When Uaica at last awoke, the sun had set and the forest was shrouded in darkness. He looked around but saw no animals nearby. He ran home as fast as he could. But the next morning he could think of

nothing but that tree and the mysterious Sinaa, the Jaguar Man, and so he walked back into the forest, telling no one where he was going.

He found the tree and all those sleeping animals. He lay down and fell fast asleep, and once again Sinaa came to him in his dream.

For days Uaica visited the forest and dreamed, and every day he learned a new secret. But he stayed later and later, and so missed many meals. As the days passed, he grew thinner and more sickly. When Jaguar Man saw this, he said to Uaica in his dream: "I have taught you enough. Now you must promise to stay away from this place. If you return, you might never leave."

Uaica took this advice deep into his heart, for he had grown to love Sinaa nearly as much as he loved his grandfather. He would be sad not to return, but he gave his word, and then he walked home.

"Child," his grandfather said, "I have been greatly worried about you. Please, you must eat."

Uaica comforted his grandfather. "Do not worry," he told the old man. "I have a secret," and then he led his grandfather into the forest to show him the Dreaming Tree.

When they were nearly there, Uaica stopped, for he remembered Sinaa's words. "I cannot go closer, grandfather. I must stay away now." But his grandfather already had walked close, and the powers of the Dreaming Tree had captured him. He was on the ground, fast asleep among the animals.

Uaica stood at a distance and watched as his grandfather slept. He longed to hear Jaguar Man's words. "Perhaps I'll move closer," he said, but he stopped himself. Uaica would never break a promise.

When at last his grandfather awoke, he hurried to Uaica's side. "You must never speak of this tree to anyone," he said. "It is a powerful tree. Those who sleep here must be strong of heart. Anyone without a strong heart might use the knowledge of the forest against our people."

When Uaica and his grandfather returned to the village, they learned that one of the boys who always teased Uaica, a boy named Casimiro, had fallen gravely ill. His family feared he would die.

"I can heal him," Uaica said, and he went to the boy's side, laid his hands upon him, and Casimiro was cured.

So it was true. Sinaa had given Uaica the gift of healing.

The villagers were amazed that this scrawny boy had special powers, and for a long time they did not believe this could be so. But again and again Uaica cured those who were ailing, and soon everyone understood Uaica had a special gift. No longer did the bullies tease him. Casimiro became one of his dearest friends.

One night Sinaa came to Uaica again in a dream. "You have done well, child," he told him. "You obeyed my command to stay away from the Dreaming Tree, and you have shown generosity to all, even your enemies. Therefore I will teach you more."

Every night after that, Jaguar Man visited Uaica in his dreams. Uaica and his grandfather built a house in which to sleep and dream, and there Uaica learned the wisdom of the forest. Along with his healing powers, he learned to work with all the forest's gifts. He created necklaces and bracelets, belts and coats using feathers and flowers, stones and shells, nuts and bones. People were dazzled by the beauty he could conjure from the smallest, simplest things.

All was well until one day greed and envy crept into the heart of a woman of the village. "There's no sense learning to create these things," she said to her friends. "Uaica owns so many wonderful things. We should steal his treasures."

They hid behind Uaica's house until he returned from fishing in the river. But Uaica had learned another secret from Jaguar Man. He could see everything, even things standing behind him, and he spied his enemies in hiding. He quickly turned on them.

"This is how you repay me?" he said. "Now your greed will rob you of gifts." And with those words he vanished beneath the crevice in a rock, and the boy who could cure all was lost to the people forever.

However, legend tells us that to this day, Uaica dreams inside that rock, where he continues to learn the gift of healing from Sinaa, the Jaguar Man. It is also said that those who possess loving and generous hearts and listen closely in their dreams may still receive his wisdom.

Friedman, Amy. "The Dreaming Tree." *SunSentinel*. Sun Sentinel, 24 Apr. 2007. Web. 17 Feb. 2016. <http://articles.sun-sentinel.com/2007-04-24/features/0704230174_1_dream-tree-forest>.

Finding the Gist and Unfamiliar Vocabulary: "The Dreaming Tree"

RL.5.4, L.5.4

Name: ______________________ **Date:** ____________

Text	Gist (What is it mostly about?)	Unfamiliar Vocabulary	Meaning (use a dictionary if you need to)
• Beginning at "Once upon a time …" • Ending at "… beside each other."			
• Beginning at "Uaica stood and stared …" • Ending at "… where he was going."			
• Beginning at "He found the tree …" • Ending at "… you must eat."			

Text	**Gist** (What is it mostly about?)	**Unfamiliar Vocabulary**	**Meaning** (use a dictionary if you need to)
• Beginning at "Uaica comforted his ..." • Ending at "against our people."			
• Beginning at "When Uaica and his grandfather ..." • Ending at "...teach you more."			
• Beginning at "Every night after that ..." • Ending at "... turned on them."			
• Beginning at "This is how ..." • Ending at "... receive his wisdom."			

Point of View Handout

RL.5.6

Name: ______________________ **Date:** __________

Describing the Point of View

The *point of view* is the narrator's position in relation to the story being told. It shows the opinion or feelings of the individuals involved in a situation. Point of view is the way the author allows the reader to "hear" and "see" what is happening.

An author chooses the point of view to use, and this influences the information given and how events are described in the story.

Point of View	What is it?	Key words	Example
first person	The narrator is a character in the story; the narrator is telling you his or her story. • makes the reader feel close to the character telling the story • helps the reader see the story through the character's eyes • what the reader knows and understands is limited to what that character knows and understands		

Point of View	What is it?	Key words	Example
third person	The narrator is not a character in the story; the narrator tells the story like a camera recording the events. • The story might be told through the experiences of a particular character or many characters. • It is possible for the reader to know and understand more than any one character could know.		

"A Walk in the Rainforest"

I was walking back to camp, gazing up at the rainforest canopy to see if I could spot any unusual birds or animals when, "CRASH!" I tripped and fell to my hands and knees on the ground! Curious, I looked around to see what I had stumbled over. "Probably just a fallen branch or an exposed tree root," I reassured myself. At first glance, I saw what looked like a branch lying on the ground in my path. There was something not quite right about it, though, and as I looked more closely, I noticed that it was hairy! And it was breathing! The cause of my fall was a tapir that was still fast asleep at my feet.

"How odd," I said to myself. As I continued to look around, things got even more strange! Curled up sleeping next to the tapir was a sloth, and next to the sloth, more animals: a monkey and a caiman. A jaguar family nestled together a little farther on, all asleep. There was even an enormous anaconda! "Yikes!" I shouted, jumping a few steps back. I knew better than to get close to some of these dangerous animals, sleeping or not.

As I took in the sleeping animals, I noticed they were congregated around a huge tree. My eyes warily wandered from the base of the tree where all the sleeping animals lay, up the trunk, to the looming branches and leaves above.

"This is all strange. Very strange indeed," I thought to myself.

740L

Written by EL Education for instructional purposes

Exit Ticket: Point of View

RL.5.6

Name: ______________________ **Date:** ____________

Directions: *Answer the question below.*

1. Read this excerpt from *The Most Beautiful Roof in the World*:

The rainforest is a timeless, unchartered world, where mysteries abound and new or rare species appear like undiscovered islands. Within the tangled vines under the rotting bark of fallen trees, caught in the slime and mold of decaying vegetation and fungi, life teems with ceaseless energy. When a tree falls, the stump rots, bark loosens, and new creatures move in and take over the altered habitats. It is the very diversity of the rainforest that allows life to thrive everywhere, to spring back with a rush of opportunistic species to fill the gaps.

Part A

From what point of view is this passage being told?

a. First person—Meg Lowman is narrating.

b. First person—An unknown narrator is narrating.

c. Third person—Meg Lowman is narrating.

d. Third person—An unknown narrator is narrating.

Part B

How does this point of view influence how the rainforest is described?

____

____

____

____

Finding the Gist and Unfamiliar Vocabulary: *The Great Kapok Tree*

RL.5.4, L.5.4

Name: ______________________ **Date:** ____________

Text	**Gist** What is it mostly about?	**Unfamiliar Vocabulary**	**Meaning** (use a dictionary if you need to)
pages 2–4 • Beginning at "Two men walked …" • Ending at "… him to sleep."			
pages 5–12 • Beginning at "A boa constrictor …" • Ending at "… smoldering ruins remain."			
pages 13–20 • Beginning at "A bright and small …" • Ending at "… world without trees."			
pages 21–24 • Beginning at "A three-toed sloth …" • Ending at "… with new eyes."			
pages 25–31 • Beginning at "The man awoke …" • Ending at "… out of the rainforest."			

Figurative Language Handout

RL.5.4, L.5.5a, L.5.5b

Figurative language is when a writer uses a word or phrase with a specific meaning that may be different from the literal meaning. Writers use figurative language to help the reader understand something new about the topic.

Writers often use figurative language to compare things in an interesting or descriptive way.

Type of figurative language	What is it?	Example
Simile	a phrase that compares two different things using the words "like" or "as"	like two peas in a pod as big as an elephant
Metaphor	a phrase that describes something by comparing it to some other thing	America is a melting pot.
Idiom	an expression that cannot be understood from the meanings of its separate words but that has a separate meaning of its own	a penny for your thoughts

Explaining Quotes: Figurative Language Note-catcher

RL.5.1, RL.5.4, L.5.5a, L.5.5b

Name: ______________________ **Date:** __________

Context	Quote	What does this help us understand?	Source
	"It is a powerful tree. Those who sleep there must be strong of heart. Anyone without **a strong heart** might use the knowledge of the forest against our people."		*"The Dreaming Tree" (a Folk Tale from Brazil)* p. 2
	"Senhor, when you awake, please **look upon us all with new eyes**."		*The Great Kapok Tree* p. 23
	"Spots of bright light **glowed like jewels** amidst the dark green forest."		*The Great Kapok Tree* p. 27
	"... The top of the rainforest at Blue Creek **looks like a field of gigantic broccoli**."		*The Most Beautiful Roof in the World* p. 13

Context	Quote	What does this help us understand?	Source
	"The sun slammed down upon the scientist **like a sledgehammer**."		*The Most Beautiful Roof in the World* p. 35
	"For those creatures that swing or glide or climb, there are **the 'emerald highways'** strung together by vines and lianas that lace the tops of the trees together into a web for commuting life."		*The Most Beautiful Roof in the World* p. 16
	"… The inner leaves are a fiery red and **erupt like tongues of flame from a volcano**."		*The Most Beautiful Roof in the World* p. 25
	"A beetle. It's beautiful. It's kind of purple—no, sort of gold. Its back **is like polished metal**, and it's got this **weird Darth Vader head on it**."		*The Most Beautiful Roof in the World* p. 33

Explaining Quotes Handout

RL.5.1, RI.5.1

Name: ______________________ **Date:** ____________

Explaining Quotes

Linking Words and Phrases for Explaining Quotes when Speaking and Writing

Context *What is happening in the text when the quote occurs?*	**Quote** *What are the exact words the author uses?*	**What does this help us understand?** *How does this quote relate to your thesis?*	**Source** *Where did this quote come from?*
• For example, in the beginning ... • Similarly ... • In one part ... • When ... • In another part ... • At the beginning of the story ... • Toward the end of the story ... • At one point ... • Later ...	**Always** record these in quotation marks. When possible, try to incorporate the author's words (in quotation marks) naturally into your sentences. OR use one of the following linking phrases: • The author tells us ... • We learn that ... • [The author] writes ... • The author describes ...	• This helps us to understand ... • This shows ... • This description shows ... • The author's description ... • This lets the reader know that ... • The author ...	Include the **title** of the text, the **author**, and the **page** number.

Exit Ticket: Explaining Quotes

RL.5.1, RL.5.4, L.5.5b

Name: ____________________ **Date:** ____________

Directions: *Answer the question below.*

1. Read this excerpt from pages 35–36 of *The Most Beautiful Roof in the World*:

The extreme heat was not the worst thing, though, in Meg's mind. Underneath the platform of the tent where she slept at night lurked one of West Africa's deadliest snakes—the Gabon viper. It did not ease her mind to be told that the snake was very shy. Once, in the middle of the night as she made her way to the outhouse, she stepped smack into a battalion of army ants. She screamed bloody murder and woke the entire camp—everyone was sure the Gabon viper had struck. But the army ants with their fierce jaws can deliver a stinging bite that is very painful.

What does the idiom "screamed bloody murder" help us to understand about Meg's experience in the rainforest?

Context	Quote	What does this help us understand?	Source

Venn Diagram : Figurative Language Graphic Organizer

RL.5.4, RL.5.9, L.5.5a,b

Name: ______________________________ **Date:** ______________

Directions: *Use the Explaining Quotes: Figurative Language note-catcher to complete this Venn diagram comparing how two of the texts you've read use figurative language.*

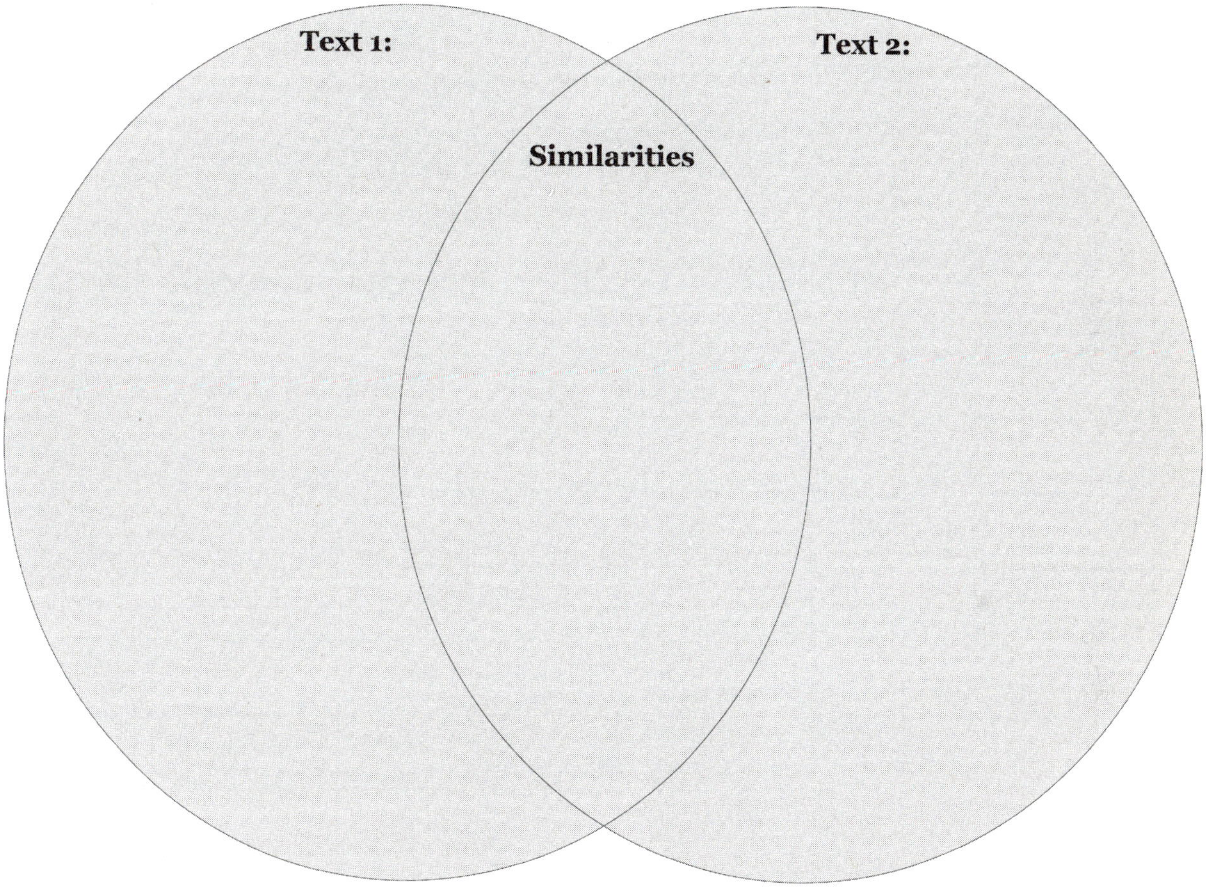

Comparison Paragraph Frame

RL.5.1, RL.5.4, RL.5.9, W.5.2, W.5.9a, L.5.2d, L.5.5a,b

Name: ______________________________ **Date:** ______________

Directions: *Use the Explaining Quotes: Figurative Language and Venn Diagram: Figurative Language graphic organizers to complete this paragraph describing a similarity in how two of the texts you've read use figurative language.*

______________________________________ and

__________________________________ both take place in the rainforest.

Although the texts are different in many ways, in both texts the author uses

_____________ to help us better understand the rainforest. For example, in

____,

when ________________________________, the author tells us

"____."

This helps us understand that ______________________________

____.

Similarly, when ____

____,

we learn

"____

____."

This description helps us understand _________________________

____.

The figurative language used by both authors helps us better understand this strange and beautiful place.

Tracking Progress: Reading, Understanding, and Explaining New Texts

R.5.1, R.5.4, R.5.10, L.5.4

Name: ______________________ **Date:** ____________

Learning Target: I can independently read, understand, and explain the meaning of a new text.

Standards I'm Tracking: RL/RI.5.1, RL.5.4, RL.5.10, L.5.4

Text Type (circle): Informative Story Poem Play/Readers Theater

1. How am I doing?

- For each criterion, self-assess by putting a check mark in the appropriate column.
- Write the number of each standard on a sticky note or flag. Then on your assessment materials, place each sticky note in an area that shows evidence you have met the criteria. This might be next to a selected response question or a short piece of writing. Make sure you have evidence for each criterion.
- Strive to be honest with yourself. Remember, your ability grows with your effort, so it's fine if you aren't there yet!

You will receive feedback on different colored sticky notes/flags and in a different colored pen on the checklist.

Reading, Understanding, and Explaining a New Text					
Standard	**Criteria for reading, understanding, and explaining a new text**	**4 On target**	**3 Getting there**	**2 Working on it**	**1 Need support**
RL.5.1/ RI.5.1	I can quote accurately to explain what a text says and to make inferences.				
RL.4.4/ RI.4.4 L.4.4	I can determine the meaning of unknown words and phrases, including figurative language, using at least one of the following strategies: Use context. Use affixes and roots. Use reference materials.				
RL.5.10/ RI.5.10	I can read and understand grade 5 level texts independently.				

2. How have I improved since I last worked on this skill?

____

____

____

Teacher Response:

____

____

____

3. How can I improve next time?

____

____

____

Teacher Response:

____

____

____

Anchor Standards:

R.1
By the end of grade 12 I will be able to: Read closely to determine what the text says explicitly and to make logical inferences from it; cite specific textual evidence when writing or speaking to support conclusions drawn from the text.

R.4
By the end of grade 12 I will be able to: Interpret words and phrases as they are used in a text, including determining technical, connotative, and figurative meanings, and analyze how specific word choices shape meaning or tone.

R.10
By the end of grade 12 I will be able to: Read and comprehend complex literary and informational texts independently and proficiently.

L.4
By the end of grade 12 I will be able to: Determine or clarify the meaning of unknown and multiple-meaning words and phrases by using context clues, analyzing meaningful word parts, and consulting general and specialized reference materials, as appropriate.

Excerpt of Pages 41–42 of *The Most Beautiful Roof in the World*

Focusing question: What does the author's use of concrete language and sensory detail help you understand about the rainforest?

Meg's voice spins out into the night. The words **dissolve** into the thick, **humid** air of the rainforest. They become meaningless sounds in the darkness. The palm viper **coiled** in the **buttressed** roots of the acacia tree might hear them, but more meaningful is the **flick** of an anole's tail on a nearby philodendron leaf. An ocelot on the prowl has passed the empty web of the slingshot spider and moves toward the strange sounds. A chameleon clamps two toes on one side of a stem and three on the other and listens to the soft burr of noise from inside, the place it cannot see. In the understory, above the chameleon, a frog slaps its sticky padded feet on a palm frond and freezes—are these the sounds of its enemy, the coati? And far overhead, in the canopy, a fruit bat cocks its **sonar** toward the dark little cabin one hundred feet below as it swoops through the night dropping a seed here, a seed there. The words, the strange sounds, melt into the night as a tiny bromeliad begins to grow in silence and invisibility high above. The bat flies on.

Glossary

dissolve: to disintegrate or scatter so as to vanish

humid: having a high amount of water vapor; damp; moist

coil: to wind in a circle

buttress: anything that gives support

buttressed: to give support to with a buttress

flick: a sharp, light snap or blow

sonar: a method for locating objects by means of transmitted and reflected sound waves (acronym for "sound navigation and ranging")

Rainforest Animals and Plants

viper: a poisonous snake with long, hollow fangs

fruit bat: any of various tropical fruit-eating bats such as the flying fox

chameleon: any of a variety of lizards capable of changing skin color to blend with the environment

ocelot: a spotted wild cat of Central and South America, similar to but smaller than a leopard

coati: a small tree-dwelling mammal, related to the raccoon, with a flexible snout and long ringed tail, found in Mexico and Central and South America

acacia tree: any of several tropical trees of the mimosa family

anole*: lizard of the iguana family that has a brightly colored dewlap and the ability to change color

Definitions from Wordsmyth online dictionary https://kids.wordsmyth.net/we/

Language Dive Note-catcher III: *The Most Beautiful Roof in the World*

[ellipsis]: the omission of words or phrases that are clearly understood from context

A chameleon clamps two toes on one side of a stem and three [ ] on the other [ ] and listens to the soft burr of noise from inside [ ], the place it cannot see.

Sketch some of the concrete language and sensory details in this sentence.

The palm viper ________ and listens to the anole, the enemy it ________.

Exit Ticket: What does the author's use of concrete language and sensory detail help you understand about the rainforest?

RL.5.4

Name: ______________________ **Date:** ______________

Choose a concrete word or phrase or an example of sensory language from the excerpt of text you read today. What did it help you to understand about the rainforest? How? Remember that concrete words and phrases are those that provide precise details and specific identifying information, and sensory details are about how things look, sound, taste, touch, and feel.

Explaining Quotes: Concrete and Sensory Language Note-catcher

RL.5.1, RL.5.4, L.5.5

Name: ______________________ **Date:** ____________

Focus question: *What does the author's use of concrete language and sensory detail help you understand about the rainforest?*

Context: *When Meg is reading a story to the boys, the author zooms outside of their cabin to what is happening in the rainforest to show how life in the rainforest responds to the sound of her voice.*

Quote	What does this help us understand?	Source

Quote	What does this help us understand?	Source

Exit Ticket: Focus Statement

W.5.2a

Name: ______________________ **Date:** ____________

"What does the author's use of concrete language and sensory detail help you understand about the rainforest?"

In pages 41–42 of *The Most Beautiful Roof in the World*, Kathryn Lasky's description of the sights and sounds of the rainforest helps the reader understand:

____

____

____

Model Essay: Concrete and Sensory Language in *The Great Kapok Tree*

Focus Question: *What does the use of concrete language and sensory detail help you understand about the rainforest?*

The Great Kapok Tree, by Lynne Cherry, is a tale about a man who goes into the rainforest with an ax to cut down a kapok tree. The man falls asleep, and in his dreams, the animals of the rainforest explain to him how losing the tree would affect their lives. Throughout the story, the author uses concrete language and sensory detail to describe events and experiences. Lynne Cherry's description of things the man hears and sees helps the reader to understand the serious consequences of cutting down the kapok tree.

The book begins with a description of sounds. When two men enter the rainforest, instantly the "sounds of squawking birds" and "howling monkeys" stop and "all was quiet as the creatures watched the two men and wondered why they had come." The sudden silence lets the reader know that the men are strangers to the forest and that the animals are worried about why they are there. When one of the men lies down to take a nap, the rainforest animals visit him in a dream to explain how the tree is important to them. The author tells us that the snake" hissed in his ear," the tree frog talked in a "squeaky voice," and the jaguar "growled in his ear," each explaining what the kapok tree meant to it. Cherry describes the sounds their voices make, as well as what they say, to help us better picture the animals that depend on the tree. Descriptions like this help us to imagine and care about the creatures in the rainforest that will lose their home and food if the tree is chopped down.

Lynne Cherry also uses description to help the reader "see" the consequences of rainforest destruction. Toward the end of the story, the toucan describes what can happen to the forest once people settle in and set fires to clear the land. He tells the man, "Where once there was life and beauty, only black and smoldering ruins remain." The author paints a visual picture for the reader, showing vividly what rainforest destruction can look like. When the man finally awakens from his long dream, the author describes the beautiful, healthy rainforest that he sees: "Spots of bright light glowed like jewels amidst the dark green forest. Strange and beautiful plants seemed to dangle in the air suspended from the great Kapok tree." Cherry's description of how the rainforest looks when it is vibrant with life contrasts with the description of how the forest could look if people are not careful. Describing the rainforest in this way helps us understand how beautiful and valuable it is.

In The Great Kapok Tree, Lynne Cherry's description does more than just show us what the rainforest looks and sounds like. Her description helps the reader to imagine how tragic it would be to lose those sights and sounds.

Source:
Lynne Cherry. *The Great Kapok Tree*. HMH Books for Young Readers, 2000.

Informative Writing Planning Graphic Organizer

W.5.2, W.5.4, W.5.5, W.5.9b

Name: ______________________ **Date:** ____________

Focus Question: What does the author's use of concrete language and sensory detail help you understand about the rainforest?

Focus Statement:

Introduction Paragraph	Proof Paragraph 1
How will you introduce the topic? What context do you need to give to your reader? • What is the title of the text? • Who is the author? State your focus:	What is one way the author's use of concrete language and sensory detail helps you understand the rainforest? Text Evidence: What facts and evidence support your focus? How? Elaboration: What does it help you to understand about the rainforest?

Proof Paragraph 2	Conclusion Paragraph
What is another way the author's use of concrete language and sensory detail helps you understand the rainforest? Text Evidence: What facts and evidence support your focus? How? Elaboration: What does it help you to understand about the rainforest?	Restate your focus statement from the introduction. Why does this matter?

My Sources: List any sources you used in planning your informative piece.	**Precise Language and Domain-Specific Vocabulary to Be Used:**

Informative Writing Checklist

Standard	Characteristics of Effective Informative Writing	Characteristics of My Literary Analysis Essay	Yes? No?
W.5.9	My focus statement shows that I clearly understand the topic or text and is well supported with evidence from reliable sources.		
W.5.2a	I provide a general observation and focus and maintain the focus consistently throughout the piece.		
W.5.2a	I introduce the topic, giving readers the context they need to understand the piece.		
W.5.2a	Information is grouped logically, in a way that makes my thinking clear to the reader.		
W.5.2a	I use formatting, illustrations, and multimedia to help the reader understand information and ideas.		
W.5.2b	I use accurate and relevant facts, definitions, concrete details, quotations, or other information and examples to explain my thinking.		

Standard	Characteristics of Effective Informative Writing	Characteristics of My Literary Analysis Essay	Yes? No?
W.5.2.c	I use linking words to show how ideas and information connect.		
W.5.2d **L.5.6**	I use precise language and domain-specific vocabulary.		
W.5.2e	I have a conclusion that is clearly related to the focus and the information presented.		
W.5.4 (partial)	My writing is appropriate for this task, purpose, and audience.		
W.5.8 (partial)	I list my sources.		
L.5.1 **L.5.3a**	My words and sentences follow the rules of writing.		
L.5.2	My spelling, capitalization, and punctuation are correct.		

Reading Fluency Checklist

	Characteristics of Fluent Reading	Symbol	4 Advanced	3 Proficient	2 Developing	1 Beginning
RF.4b,c	I can read all/almost all of the words correctly.					
RF.4c	I can correct myself and reread when what I read was wrong or didn't make sense.					
RF.4a,b	I can read at a speed that is appropriate for the piece.					
RF.4a,b	I can read smoothly without many breaks.					
RF.4a,b	I can read groups of related words and phrases together.					
RF.4a,b	I can notice and read punctuation. (Examples: Pauses after a comma and period, questions sound like questions, dialogue sounds like someone saying it, exclamations in an excited voice)					
RF.4b	I can use the appropriate tone to express the author's meaning.					
RF.4b	I can use facial expressions and body language to match the expression in my voice.					
RF.4b	I can use the appropriate volume and change volume naturally as if I am talking to a friend.					

Linking Words and Phrases

W.5.1c, W.5.2c, W.5.3c

Add to this chart if you find new linking words and phrases you would like to remember.

Temporal words and phrases (Time order)	Words and phrases that connect ideas
first	also
second	another
next	and
finally	but
then	more
lastly	for example
in the end	as you can see
after that	in addition
	consequently
	specifically
	in contrast
	especially
	furthermore

Entry Ticket: Guess the Focus Statement

W.3.2a

A good conclusion restates the focus statement of the piece and adds some reflection on the information and ideas presented in the piece. Below is a conclusion taken from an essay written about the rainforest. With a partner, read the conclusion and try to figure out what the focus statement of the essay could have been. Ask yourselves what "big idea" is restated in this paragraph. Then try writing a possible focus statement for the essay in the space provided.

In The Most Beautiful Roof in the World, *Katherine Lasky's description does more than just show the reader how the rainforest looks and sounds. Her description helps us understand the amazing diversity of life in the rainforest and reminds us that humans are just one small part of that.*

Possible focus statement for this essay:

____

____

____

____

____

Tracking Progress: Informative Writing

Name: ______________________________ **Date:** ______________

Learning Target: I can write an informative text.

Standard I'm Tracking: W.5.2

1. How am I doing?
   - For each criterion, self-assess by putting a check mark in the appropriate column.
   - Write the number of each standard on a sticky note or flag. Then on your own writing, place each sticky note in an area that shows evidence you have met that criterion. Make sure you have evidence for each criterion.
   - Strive to be honest with yourself. Remember, your ability grows with your effort, so it's fine if you aren't there yet!

You will receive feedback on different colored sticky notes/flags and in a different colored pen on the checklist.

Standard	Characteristics of an Effective Informative Piece	4 Advanced	3 Proficient	2 Developing	1 Beginning
***W.5.9**	My focus shows that I clearly understand the topic or text and is well supported with evidence from reliable sources.				
***W.5.2a**	I provide a general observation and focus and maintain the focus consistently throughout the piece.				
***W.5.2a**	I introduce the topic, giving readers the context they need to understand the piece.				
W.5.2e	I have a conclusion that is clearly related to the focus and the information presented.				

Standard	Characteristics of an Effective Informative Piece	4 Advanced	3 Proficient	2 Developing	1 Beginning
***W.5.2a**	Information is grouped logically, in a way that makes my thinking clear to the reader.				
W.5.2c	I use linking words to show how ideas and information connect.				
W.5.2b	I use accurate and relevant facts, definitions, concrete details, quotations, or other information and examples to explain my thinking.				
W.5.2a	I use formatting, illustrations, and multimedia to help the reader understand information and ideas.				
W.5.2d **L.5.6**	I use precise language and domain-specific vocabulary.				
W.5.4 (partial) **W.5.3a**	My writing is appropriate for this purpose and audience.				
W.5.8 (partial)	I list my sources.				
L.5.1 **L.5.3a**	My words and sentences follow the rules of writing.				
L.5.2	The spelling, capitalization, and punctuation are correct.				

2. How have I improved since I last worked on this skill?

____

____

____

Teacher Response:

____

____

____

3. How can I improve next time?

____

____

____

Teacher Response:

____

____

____

Anchor Standard: W.2

By the end of Grade 12 I will be able to: Write informative/explanatory texts to examine and convey complex ideas and information clearly and accurately through the effective selection, organization, and analysis of content.

Grade 5: Module 2: Unit 2

Homework Resources (for Families)

Unit 2: Analyzing Author's Craft

Common Core State Standards addressed: RL.5.1, RL.5.4, RL.5.6, W.5.2, W.5.4, W.5.9a, RL.5.9, L.5.2d, L.5.5a,b

Guiding Questions and Big Ideas

How does a narrator's or speaker's point of view influence how events are described?

- *A first person narrative helps us to see exactly how one character thinks and feels in response to a situation, while a third person narrative helps us to understand the thoughts and feelings of more than one character.*

How do authors engage the reader in narratives?

- *Authors engage the reader in narratives by using concrete and sensory language to help readers imagine they are there.*

What will your child be doing at school?

In this unit, students read and analyze literary texts, focusing on how the point of view influences the way events in the text are described and how concrete and descriptive language help a reader to understand a text. Students read several literary texts about the rainforest, including "The Dreaming Tree," a folk tale from Brazil, *The Great Kapok Tree*, and excerpts of *The Most Beautiful Roof in the World*. In the first half of the unit, they compare the point of view and figurative language used in these texts and in *The Most Beautiful Roof in the World*. In the mid-unit assessment, students read and analyze a new literary text. In the second half of the unit, students analyze the use of concrete and sensory language in an excerpt of *The Most Beautiful Roof in the World* and what it helps the reader understand. They work in pairs to write a literary analysis essay to answer the question: What does the use of concrete language and sensory detail help you understand about the rainforest? In the end of unit assessment, they read a new excerpt of *The Most Beautiful Roof in the World* and independently write a literary analysis essay to answer the same question. Throughout the second half of the unit, students also practice reading aloud new excerpts of *The Most Beautiful Roof in the World* in preparation for a reading fluency assessment at the end of the unit.

The Language standards that students will focus on in this unit (L.5.5a, L5.5b) require them to interpret figurative language, such as similes and metaphors, in the context of the text (L.5.5a) and to recognize and explain the meaning of common idioms (L.5.5b).

The **point of view** is the narrator's position in relation to the story being told. It shows the opinion or feelings of the individuals involved in a situation. Point of view is the way the author allows the reader to "hear" and "see" what is happening.

In **first person point of view**, the narrator is a character in the story; the narrator is telling you his or her story. This makes the reader feel close to the character telling the story and helps the reader see the story through the character's eyes. What the reader knows and understands is limited to what that character knows and understands.

In **third person point of view**, the narrator is not a character in the story; the narrator tells the story like a camera recording the events. The story might be told through the experiences of a particular character or many characters, and it is possible for the reader to know and understand more than any one character could know.

Interpreting Figurative Language

Figurative language is when a writer uses a word or phrase with a specific meaning that may be different from the literal meaning. Writers use figurative language to help the reader understand something new about the topic.

Writers often use figurative language to compare things in an interesting or descriptive way.

Type of Figurative Language	What is it?	Example
simile	a phrase that compares two different things using the words "like" or "as"	like two peas in a pod as big as an elephant
metaphor	a phrase that describes something by comparing it to some other thing	America is a melting pot.
idiom	an expression that cannot be understood from the meanings of its separate words but has a separate meaning of its own	a penny for your thoughts

Concrete and Sensory Language

	Definition and Function
Sensory details	*details that describe for the reader how things look, sound, feel, smell, and taste, so that readers can imagine the experience as if they were there*
Concrete words and phrases	*These provide precise details and specific identifying information to give your mind something solid to imagine when you read a sentence. Concrete words and phrases often precisely describe sensory experiences (how things look, smell, taste, feel, sound).*

How can you support your child at home?

- Talk to your child about the texts he or she is reading and the types of figurative language the authors use.
- Talk to your child about what the figurative language the authors use helps him or her to understand about the text.
- Read first and third person narratives and encourage your child to identify the point of view and any figurative language used.
- When reading narratives with your child, invite him or her to identify any concrete and sensory language and to explain what it helps the reader to understand.

Unit 2: Homework

In Lessons 1–4, homework focuses on research reading and vocabulary.

In Lessons 5–13, homework focuses on analyzing the concrete and sensory language in independent reading texts and practicing reading excerpts of *The Most Beautiful Roof in the World* aloud.

Research reading: Your child is expected to independently research the topic by reading topic-related books of his or her choice for approximately 20 minutes **each day** and responding to a prompt of choice in the **front** of the independent reading journal. These are usually books your child will bring home from school; however, they may be topic-related books chosen by the child at the public or home library. Prompts for independent reading can be found in the homework materials provided.

Choice reading: If your child would also like to independently read and respond to a book of free choice, he or she may use the **back** of the independent reading journals. Prompts for independent reading can be found in the homework materials provided.

Lesson	Lesson Content	Homework Practice	Due In	Anticipated Date*
1	Students describe the point of view in two literary texts.	1. Research reading and answering prompt.	1. Teacher will check independent reading journals strategically.	
2	Students analyze the figurative language used in quotes from literary texts.	1. Vocabulary 2. For ELLs: Language Dive II Part 1 Practice 3. Research reading and answering prompt	1. **Lesson 5** 2. **Lesson 3** 3. Teacher will check independent reading journals strategically.	
3	Students compare the figurative language used in two literary texts.	1. Vocabulary 2. Research reading and answering prompt	1. **Lesson 5** 2. Teacher will check independent reading journals strategically.	
4	Students work independently to read and analyze the point of view and figurative language in a new literary text for the mid-unit assessment.	1. Vocabulary 2. Research reading and answering prompt	1. **Lesson 5** 2. Teacher will check independent reading journals strategically.	
5	Students closely read a new excerpt of *The Most Beautiful Roof in the World.*	1. Research reading and answering prompt 2. For ELLs: Language Dive III Practice	1. Teacher will check independent reading journals strategically. 2. **Lesson 6**	
6	Students analyze the excerpt of *The Most Beautiful Roof in the World* read closely in the previous lesson for concrete and sensory language.	1. Gathering concrete and sensory language from independent reading texts 2. Research reading and answering prompt	1. **Lesson 8** 2. Teacher will check independent reading journals strategically.	
7	Students analyze a model literary analysis and choose a focus statement for their own literary analysis.	1. Gathering concrete and sensory language from independent reading texts 2. Research reading and answering prompt	1. **Lesson 8** 2. Teacher will check independent reading journals strategically.	

* Teacher note: Please complete the Anticipated Date column according to your schedule.

Lesson	Lesson Content	Homework Practice	Due In	Anticipated Date*
8	Students analyze the introduction of the model literary analysis essay and work with a partner to write the introduction to their own literary analysis essay.	1. Choose an excerpt of *The Most Beautiful Roof in the World* to read aloud. 2. Research reading and answering prompt	1. **Lessons 12 and 13** 2. Teacher will check independent reading journals strategically.	
9	Students analyze the first body paragraph of the model literary analysis essay and then work with a partner to write the first body paragraph of their own literary analysis essay.	1. Choose an excerpt of *The Most Beautiful Roof in the World* to read aloud. 2. Research reading and answering prompt	1. **Lessons 12 and 13** 2. Teacher will check independent reading journals strategically.	
10	Students analyze the second body paragraph of the model literary analysis essay and then work with a partner to write the second body paragraph of their own literary analysis essay.	1. Choose an excerpt of *The Most Beautiful Roof in the World* to read aloud. 2. Research reading and answering prompt	1. **Lessons 12 and 13** 2. Teacher will check independent reading journals strategically.	
11	Students analyze the conclusion of the model literary analysis essay and then work with a partner to write the conclusion of their own literary analysis essay.	1. Choose an excerpt of *The Most Beautiful Roof in the World* to read aloud. 2. Research reading and answering prompt	1. **Lessons 12 and 13** 2. Teacher will check independent reading journals strategically.	
12+13	Students complete the End of Unit 2 Assessment, in which they read a new excerpt of *The Most Beautiful Roof in the World* and write a literary analysis essay.	1. Research reading and answering prompt	1. Teacher will check independent reading journals strategically.	

*Teacher note: Please complete the Anticipated Date column according to your schedule.

Independent Reading

Independent Reading Prompts

Directions: Remember to record responses to **research reading in the front** of your independent reading journal and responses to **choice reading in the back**. Try to choose a different prompt each time.

Record any new vocabulary in your vocabulary log. Remember, academic vocabulary is recorded in the front, and domain-specific vocabulary (words about the topic) is recorded in the back. Mark vocabulary found during independent reading with a symbol—an asterisk (*), for example.

Record:

- Date
- Title and author of your reading book
- Pages you have read
- Prompt
- Response

Example:

Date: 04/08/2018

Book Title and Author: *The Most Beautiful Roof in the World* by Kathryn Lasky

Pages Read: 22-27

Prompt: What questions do you have about the rainforest canopy after reading?

Response: What other animals and plants live in the rainforest canopy?

1. **Record two or three facts in your own words about the rainforest or rainforest animals that you found out in your research reading today.**
2. **What questions do you have about the rainforest or rainforest animals after reading?**
3. **What would you like to research further after reading? Why?**
4. **Summarize your research reading today in no more than four sentences.**
5. **How would you describe the setting of the particular part of the text you read?**
   A. Hint: What did you picture in your mind as you were reading it? Why?
   B. Hint: What did it say in the text to make you think that?

6. **What do you think is going to happen next? Why?**
   A. Hint: What has the author written so far to make you think that?
7. **Summarize the pages you just read in no more than four sentences.**
8. **What is the main idea of the part of the text you just read?**
   A. Hint: The main idea is the point the author wants you to understand.
9. **Think about the title of your text. Why do you think the author chose this title?**
   A. Hint: Explain how the title fits the book.
   B. Hint: Start out: "The title of my book is. . . . The author chose this title because. . . ."
10. **What are two new words you learned in this text? Tell about the words.**
11. **Choose a picture, chart, graph, or diagram from your text. Explain how the information you learned from the image helped you understand the text.**
    A. Hint: First, think about the main idea of what you just read. Then, think about how the picture, chart, graph, or diagram supports the main idea.

Vocabulary

Directions:

In the classroom, you have been recording words from your research in your vocabulary log. Throughout this unit, you have been research reading topic-related books at home to build your knowledge of the rainforest and recording words in your independent reading journal.

You have also been learning how to interpret figurative language.

Choose a word or phrase from your research reading or from a text you've read in class and add the word or phrase to your vocabulary log. Try to choose a different word or phrase to add and to practice a different vocabulary strategy each time. For each word, be sure to add the following:

- the definition, or meaning, of the word
- the vocabulary strategy you used to figure out the meaning of the word
- a sketch or diagram that helps you to better understand the meaning of the word
- (for figurative language) the meaning of the phrase and what it helps you to understand about the text

As a reminder, the vocabulary strategies we've been working on in class are:

Vocabulary Strategies

- Context: Read the sentence around the word.
- Look at the affixes for clues.
- Look at the root of the word for clues.
- Use a dictionary.
- Discuss the word with another person (after attempting some of the above strategies).

Homework: Language Dive II Part 1 Practice

Name: ______________________ **Date:** ____________

1. The mystery quote below is scrambled. Write it in the correct sequence:

strung together by vines and lianas	that swing or glide or climb,	into a web for commut-ing life.	For those creatures	that lace the tops of the trees together	there are the "emerald highways"

____

____

____

____

2. Sketch the meaning of the mystery quote above.

3. Circle the metaphor in the mystery quote above. What is the author comparing?
   The author is comparing ______________________.

4. Draw a box around the two words used to talk about animals.

5. Underline the words and phrases that are used to talk about connecting things together.

6. Write the mystery quote above as two sentences instead of one:

____

____

____

____

7. Complete the sentence with your own ideas.

   For those creatures that________________________________,

   there are ______________________________________.

Homework: Language Dive III Practice

Name: ______________________ **Date:** ____________

1. The sentence below is scrambled. Write it in the correct sequence:

and listens to the soft burr of noise from inside,	and three on the other	on one side of a stem	the place it cannot see.	A chame-leon clamps two toes

____

____

____

____

2. Sketch the meaning of the sentence above.

3. The author used ellipsis in the sentence above. (She left out words that readers can figure out themselves.) In the brackets, write in the words she left out:

A chameleon clamps two toes on one side of a stem and three [____________] on the other [____________] and listens to the soft burr of noise from inside [_____________], [_____________] the place it cannot see.

4. Use ellipsis. Rewrite the sentence below, leaving out the words in brackets, which readers can figure out.

   The insect sees an empty web, [which is] the home of the sling-shot spider, but [the insect] gets caught [in the web].

   ____

   ____

   ____

5. Circle four words that the writer can leave out of the sentence below. Remember, the sentence has to still be clear.

   An ocelet eats a rabbit and caught five more rabbits, which is unusual.

Homework: Concrete and Sensory Language I

Name: ______________________ **Date:** ____________

Context	Quote	What does this help us understand?	Source

Homework: Concrete and Sensory Language II

Name: ______________________________ **Date:** ______________

Context	Quote	What does this help us understand?	Source

Homework: Reading Fluency: Excerpts of *The Most Beautiful Roof in the World*

Page	Excerpt beginning at	Excerpt ending at

Grade 5: Module 2

Unit 3

"Bite at Night"

I was having a dream about working on the inflatable raft in the afternoon heat. I was floating above the rainforest canopy, attached by my harness, and I was sampling leaves on the emergent layer. I was just reaching for another leaf when suddenly there was a loud bang. I woke up with a start and sat up suddenly, my heart pounding. It was pitch black as I looked around, and I couldn't figure out where I was or what I was doing there. It took me a few moments to realize that I wasn't on the inflatable raft after all. I was in my tent, it was the middle of the night, and a loud noise had woken me up. I could still hear the rustling of something moving around nearby. "Calm down, you silly thing," I said to myself, "it's only a creature foraging for a midnight snack!"

I lay back again and spent the next thirty minutes tossing and turning, trying to get back to sleep. Eventually, I determined that to go back to sleep, I needed first to visit the bathroom. The bathroom was in an outhouse a short walk from my tent. One thing I always worried about when walking around in Cameroon, particularly in the dark, was the Gabon viper, one of West Africa's deadliest snakes. I knew that at least one of those venomous snakes slept under the platform of my tent, and I certainly didn't want to run into one of them at night.

Quickly, I threw on some clothes and started walking toward the outhouse, listening intently for the sound of a snake slithering through foliage toward me. Clumsy from sleep, I caught my foot on something and nearly fell to my knees. I didn't want to put my hands on the ground, for fear of touching something sinister. I managed to save myself without touching anything and muttered under my breath, "Yikes! For goodness sake, woman, be more careful." I was wide awake now and chastised myself for not bringing my flashlight.

A few steps later, I could just make out the outline of the outhouse about 100 feet away, exposed by the rays of moonlight that were penetrating the gaps in the dense canopy. I relaxed a little to know I was nearly there.

Suddenly, I felt a sharp, searing, bite-like pain on my right ankle. "Ouch! What was that?" I gasped with surprise. I was reaching down to try to touch it when I felt it again, this time in a different spot further down my foot. In a matter of milliseconds, my entire lower leg and foot felt as though they were on fire. It felt like a thousand burning-hot needles were repeatedly being stabbed into my skin. Then it started on the other leg too. Very quickly, the pain was so intense that I couldn't think about anything else. The pain consumed me. I forgot that it was the middle of the night and everyone else in the camp would be sleeping. I started to jump up and down, hopping from one foot to the other. "Oh my goodness, owwwwwwwwwwwwwwwww!" I screamed. "Owwwwwwwww, owwwwwwww, owwwwwwww!"

After the initial shock, I began to regain my senses and became aware of the noise of people in the camp waking up and calling out to one another, "Oh no! It sounds like she's been bitten by the Gabon viper. This could be bad!" I heard the footsteps of people running toward me and saw lights flicking on and getting brighter as they approached. I caught glimpses of concerned faces in the flashlight beams.

Even though I was in a lot of pain, I realized that I needed to alleviate their concerns immediately. "Calm down, everyone," I shouted. "It's nothing to worry about. I stumbled into a battalion of army ants who are eating me alive. I was startled and it hurts, but I'm going to be all right."

I heard the grunts of displeasure as they all understood that I had awakened them for no reason, and most people started to head back to their tents. Someone loaned me a flashlight so that I could safely make it to the outhouse and then back to my tent, where I located my first aid kit and nursed my wounds.

900L

Written by EL Education for instructional purposes

Finding the Gist and Unfamiliar Vocabulary: "Bite at Night"

RL.5.4, L.5.4

Name: ____________________ **Date:** ____________

Text	**Gist** What is it mostly about?	**Unfamiliar Vocabulary**	**Meaning** (use a dictionary if you need to)
• Beginning at "I was having a dream ..." • Ending at "... a midnight snack!"			
• Beginning at "I lay back again ..." • Ending at "... them at night."			
• Beginning at "Quickly, I threw on ..." • Ending at "... I was nearly there."			
• Beginning at "Suddenly, I felt ..." • Ending at "... owwwwwwwww, owwwwww!"			
• Beginning at "After the initial shock ..." • Ending at "... nursed my wounds."			

Narrative Writing Checklist

W.5.2, W.5.4, W.5.9, L.5.1, L.5.2, L.5.3, L.5.6

Name: ______________________ **Date:** __________

Standard	Characteristics of Effective Narrative Writing	Characteristics of My First Person Rainforest Narrative	Yes? No?
W.5.9	I use information from sources to craft the characters, setting, or events in my story.		
W.5.3.a	The events in my narrative are clear and connected.		
W.5.3.a	I use details and description to introduce the narrator and establish the situation.		
W.5.3a	My narrative has a central problem.		
W.5.3a	I organize events in a sequence that unfolds naturally.		
W.5.3b	I use dialogue and description to show what characters are doing, thinking, and feeling and how they respond to situations.		

Standard	Characteristics of Effective Narrative Writing	Characteristics of My First Person Rainforest Narrative	Yes? No?
W.5.3b	I "slow down" important events by adding detail and use transitions to "speed up" events that are not important.		
W.5.3c	I use a variety of transitional words and phrases to show the sequence of events.		
W.5.3d **L.5.3 (partial)** **L.5.6**	I include sensory details and choose words carefully to help the reader imagine experiences or events.		
W.5.3e	My narrative has a satisfying conclusion.		
W.5.4 **L.5.3 (partial)**	I use a narrative voice that is appropriate to the story I'm telling and engages the reader.		
L.5.1	My words and sentences follow the rules of writing.		
L.5.2	The spelling, capitalization, and punctuation are correct.		

Narrative Planning Graphic Organizer: Partner Narrative

W.5.3, W.5.4, W.5.5

Name: ______________________ **Date:** ____________

Beginning	Middle
 *Establish a situation.* • What is happening? • What is the setting?  *Introduce the characters.* • Who is the narrator? • What does the reader need to know about him/her?	 *Describe a problem.* • What is the problem?  *Explain how the character(s) respond to the problem.* • What does the **narrator** think, feel, or do when the problem occurs? • What does he/she say?

Middle	End
• What do other **characters** think, feel, or do? • What do they say?	*Provide a solution/resolution.* • How is the problem solved/resolved?

Coordinating and Subordinating Conjunctions Handout

L.5.1a

Name: ______________________ **Date:** ____________

	Function?	Examples
Coordinating conjunctions	Coordinating conjunctions join equal words, phrases, and independent clauses. None is dependent on the other.	FANBOYS—for, and, nor, but, or, yet, so 1. I like cake, but I don't like frosting. 2. We have a big soccer game on Friday, so I am nervous.
Subordinating conjunctions	Subordinating conjunctions join two clauses together but in doing so make one clause dependent on the other.	because, when, while, though 1. We have an umbrella because it is raining. 2. Because it is raining, we have an umbrella.

Exit Ticket: Narrator's Response

W.5.3a, W.5.3b

Name: ______________________________ **Date:** ______________

Directions: *Answer the questions below.*

1. A student has written a first person narrative about the rainforest. Read this paragraph from the narrative and answer the question that follows.

In the rays of moonlight that were penetrating the gaps in the dense canopy, I could just make out the outline of the outhouse about 100 feet away. I relaxed a little to know I was nearly there. Suddenly, I felt a sharp, stinging bite on my ankle. It was immediately followed by another and another. I jumped up and down. "Owwwwwwwwwwwwwwww!" I screamed. "Owwwwwwwww, owwwwwwww, owwwwwwww!"

The student needs to fix the beginning by showing how the narrator responds to the problem. Which sentences would **best** fit in this paragraph?

a. "Oh no," someone in camp shouted. "Meg is hurt!"

b. "What in the world?" I wondered to myself. "What is biting me?"

c. "Here, take my flashlight!" she said. "And my first aid kit!"

Tracking Progress: Narrative Writing

Name: ______________________ **Date:** ____________

Learning Target: I can write a narrative text.

Standard I'm Tracking: W.5.3

1. How am I doing?

- For each criterion, self-assess by putting a check mark in the appropriate column.
- Write the number of each standard on a sticky note or flag. Then on your own writing, place each sticky note in an area that shows evidence you have met the criterion. Make sure you have evidence for each one.
- Strive to be honest with yourself. Remember, your ability grows with your effort, so it's fine if you aren't there yet!

You will receive feedback on different colored sticky notes/flags and in a different colored pen on the checklist.

Informative Writing Checklist: What Makes a Good Narrative Piece?					
Standard	**Characteristics of an Effective Narrative Piece**	**4 On target**	**3 Getting there**	**2 Working on it**	**1 Need support**
***W.5.9 RI.5.1**	I effectively use information from sources to craft the characters, setting, or events in the story.				
W.5.3a	Events in the narrative are clear and connected.				
W.5.3a	I use details and description to introduce the reader to the narrator, setting, and situation.				
W.5.3a	My narrative has a central problem.				

Informative Writing Checklist: What Makes a Good Narrative Piece?					
Standard	**Characteristics of an Effective Narrative Piece**	**4 On target**	**3 Getting there**	**2 Working on it**	**1 Need support**
W.5.3e	The narrative has a satisfying conclusion.				
W.5.3a	I organize events in a sequence that unfolds naturally.				
W.5.3c	I use a variety of transitional words and phrases to show the sequence of events.				
W.5.3b	I use dialogue and description to show what characters are doing, thinking, and feeling and how they respond to situations. I "slow down" important events by adding detail and "speed up" events that are not important.				
W.5.3d **L.5.3 (partial)**	I include sensory details and choose words carefully to help the reader imagine experiences or events.				
***W.5.4 L.5.3 (partial)**	I use a narrative voice that is appropriate to the story I'm telling and engages the reader.				
L.5.1	My words and sentences follow the rules of writing.				
L.5.2	The spelling, capitalization, and punctuation are correct.				

2. How have I improved since I last worked on this skill?

____

____

____

Teacher Response:

____

____

____

3. How can I improve next time?

____

____

____

Teacher Response:

____

____

____

Anchor Standard: W.3

By the end of Grade 12 I will be able to: Write narratives to develop real or imagined experiences or events using effective technique, well-chosen details, and well-structured event sequences.

Combining/Reducing Sentences

L.5.3a

- Someone loaned me a flashlight, so I went to the outhouse to use the bathroom. After that, I started my walk back to my tent. I walked more carefully this time to avoid falling over. Once I got back to my tent, I spent ten minutes looking for my first aid kit. I put ointment on my ant bites to soothe the pain.
- Someone loaned me a flashlight so that I could safely make it to the outhouse and then back to my tent, where I located my first aid kit and nursed my wounds.

Expanding Sentences with Concrete Words and Sensory Details

W.5.3d

1a. Suddenly, I felt pain in my right ankle.

1b. Suddenly, I felt a sharp, searing, bite-like pain on my right ankle.

2a. The sky at sunset was beautiful.

2b. The sky at sunset was purple with clouds that created streaks of yellow, orange, and pink. It was beautiful.

3a. The moon looked amazing in the sky.

Expand the sentence above with concrete words and sensory details.

Writing Dialogue Handout

W.5.3b

- Quotation marks around the actual words the character said.
- Comma at the end of speech when the sentence isn't finished.
- Comma before speech to show speech is coming.
- Punctuation (period, comma, exclamation mark, etc.) within the quotation marks.
- Capital letter at the beginning of the words that were spoken.
- New paragraphs are started when a different character is speaking.

Prepositions

L.5.1a

Key: <u>underlined</u> = preposition

A. I was having a dream <u>about</u> working <u>on</u> the inflatable raft <u>in</u> the afternoon heat.

B. I was floating <u>above</u> the rainforest canopy, attached <u>by</u> my harness, and I was sampling leaves <u>on</u> the emergent layer.

C. I was just reaching <u>for</u> another leaf when suddenly there was a loud bang.

Questions for discussion:

- What do prepositions come before?
- What is the function of a preposition?

Exit Ticket: Prepositions and Interjections

L.5.1a

Name: ______________________________ **Date:** ______________

1. Underline the prepositions in this sentence:

   It took me a few moments to realize that I wasn't on the inflatable raft after all.

2. Underline the correct answer to this question:

   What is the function of the preposition in this sentence?

   - introduces information about when
   - Introduces information about where
   - introduces information about how

3. Suggest an interjection and use the appropriate punctuation:

   ________________ That cake is delicious!

4. Underline the correct answer to this question:

   What is the function of the interjection in this sentence?

   - expresses anger
   - expresses enjoyment
   - expresses disgust

Conjunctions, Interjections, and Prepositions

L.5.1a

Name: ______________________________ **Date:** ____________

Directions: *Read the following paragraph from "Bite at Night" and answer the questions below.*

Quickly, I threw on some clothes and started walking **toward** the outhouse, listening intently **for** the sound of a snake slithering **through** foliage toward me. Clumsy from sleep, I caught my foot **on** something *and* nearly fell to my knees. I didn't want to put my hands on the ground, *for* fear of touching something sinister. I managed to save myself without touching anything *and* muttered under my breath, "For goodness sake, woman, be more careful." I was wide awake now *and* chastised myself for not bringing my flashlight.

Question 1: Add an appropriate interjection at the beginning of the dialogue. Remember to punctuate it correctly. Remember also that an interjection expresses a sudden emotional reaction (**L.5.1a**):

"______________For goodness sake, woman, be more careful."

1b. Why did you choose that interjection? What is the function of the interjection you have chosen (**L.5.1a**)?

____

____

Question 2: Some words have been highlighted in bold. What kind of words are they? Underline the correct answer.

A. interjections
B. conjunctions
C. nouns
D. prepositions

Question 3: What is the function of the word *toward* in the first sentence? Underline the correct answer:

A. to introduce information to the reader about where she was going
B. to introduce information to the reader about when she was going
C. to introduce information to the reader about how she was going

Question 4: Circle the conjunctions in the sentence (**L.5.1a**).

Question 5: Choose one conjunction and draw a box around it. What is the function of this conjunction? Why has it been used (**L.5.1a**)?

____

____

Tracking Progress: Narrative Writing

Name: ______________________ **Date:** ____________

Learning Target: I can write a narrative text.

Standard I'm Tracking: W.5.3

1. How am I doing?

- For each criterion, self-assess by putting a check mark in the appropriate column.
- Write the number of each standard on a sticky note or flag. Then on your own writing, place each sticky note in an area that shows evidence you have met the criterion. Make sure you have evidence for each criterion.
- Strive to be honest with yourself. Remember, your ability grows with your effort, so it's fine if you aren't there yet!

You will receive feedback on different colored sticky notes/flags and in a different colored pen on the checklist.

Standard	Characteristics of an Effective Narrative	4 Advanced	3 Proficient	2 Developing	1 Beginning
W.5.9 **RI.5.1**	I effectively use information from sources to craft the characters, setting, or events in the story.				
W.5.3a	Events in the narrative are clear and connected.				
W.5.3a	I use details and description to introduce the reader to the narrator, setting, and situation.				
W.5.3a	My narrative has a central problem.				
W.5.3e	The narrative has a satisfying conclusion.				

Standard	Characteristics of an Effective Narrative	4 Advanced	3 Proficient	2 Developing	1 Beginning
W.5.3a	I organize events in a sequence that unfolds naturally.				
***W.5.3c**	I use a variety of transitional words and phrases to show the sequence of events.				
***W.5.3b**	I use dialogue and description to show what characters are doing, thinking, and feeling and how they respond to situations. I "slow down" important events by adding detail and "speed up" events that are not important.				
***W.5.3d L.5.3 (partial)**	I include sensory details and choose words carefully to help the reader imagine experiences or events.				
W.5.4 L.5.3 (partial)	I use a narrative voice that is appropriate to the story I'm telling and engages the reader.				
L.5.1	My words and sentences follow the rules of writing.				
L.5.2	The spelling, capitalization, and punctuation are correct.				

2. How have I improved since I last worked on this skill?

____

____

____

Teacher Response:

____

____

____

3. How can I improve next time?

____

____

____

Teacher Response:

____

____

____

Anchor Standard: W.3

By the end of Grade 12 I will be able to: Write narratives to develop real or imagined experiences or events using effective technique, well-chosen details and well-structured event sequences

Informative Writing Checklist

Name: ______________________ **Date:** ____________

Standard	Characteristics of Effective Informative Writing	Characteristics of My ebook Author's Note	Yes? No?
W.5.9	My focus statement shows that I clearly understand the topic or text and is well supported with evidence from reliable sources.		
W.5.2a	I provide a general observation and focus and maintain the focus consistently throughout the piece.		
W.5.2a	I introduce the topic, giving readers the context they need to understand the piece.		
W.5.2a	Information is grouped logically, in a way that makes my thinking clear to the reader.		
W.5.2a	I use formatting, illustrations, and multimedia to help the reader understand information and ideas.		
W.5.2b	I use accurate and relevant facts, definitions, concrete details, quotations, or other information and examples to explain my thinking.		

Standard	Characteristics of Effective Informative Writing	Characteristics of My ebook Author's Note	Yes? No?
W.5.2.c	I use linking words to show how ideas and information connect.		
W.5.2d L.5.6	I use precise language and domain-specific vocabulary.		
W.5.2e	I have a conclusion that is clearly related to the focus and the information presented.		
W.5.4 (partial)	My writing is appropriate for this task, purpose, and audience.		
W.5.8 (partial)	I list my sources.		
L.5.1 L.5.3a	My words and sentences follow the rules of writing.		
L.5.2	My spelling, capitalization, and punctuation are correct.		

Grade 5: Module 2: Unit 3

Homework Resources (for Families)

Unit 3: Using Writing to Entertain

Common Core State Standards addressed: W.5.3, W.5.4, W.5.5, L.5.1a, L.5.3a

Guiding Questions and Big Ideas

How does a narrator's or speaker's point of view influence how events are described?

- *A first person narrative helps us to see exactly how one character thinks and feels in response to a situation, while a third person narrative helps us to understand the thoughts and feelings of more than one character.*

How do authors engage the reader in narratives?

- *Authors engage the reader in narratives by speeding up and slowing down the pacing according to what is happening.*

What will your student be doing at school?

In this unit, students apply what they have learned about point of view and narrative techniques to write a first person narrative that builds out a scenario from the anchor text for the module, *The Most Beautiful Roof in the World.* Students will work in pairs to plan and draft a partner narrative in the first half of the unit, which they will then revise in the second half of the unit, speeding up parts of the narrative that are irrelevant to the plot and slowing down important action. In the mid-unit assessment, students plan and draft a new first person narrative independently, and in the end of unit assessment they revise this narrative. Students finish the module by working with a partner to create a Rainforest Adventures ebook for their partner narrative and their two individual narratives.

The Language standards that students focus on in this unit (L.5.1a and L.5.3a) require them to identify the function of conjunctions, interjections, and prepositions in a sentence (L.5.1a) and to expand, reduce, and combine sentences for meaning (L.5.3a).

A **first person narrative** is one written from the viewpoint of a character writing or speaking directly about themselves using "I."

Conjunctions, Interjections, and Prepositions.

Part of speech	What is it?	Examples
conjunction	combines/joins together words, phrases, or clauses	Coordinating conjunctions: FANBOYS—for, and, nor, but, or, yet, so "I knew that at least one of those venomous snakes slept under the platform of my tent, and I certainly didn't want to run into one of them at night." Subordinating conjunctions: because, when, while, though "I was just reaching for another leaf when suddenly there was a loud bang."
interjection	expresses a sudden emotional reaction, such as surprise, disgust, joy, or excitement and is often found at the beginning of dialogue; often followed by an exclamation mark	Ouch! Yikes! "Ouch! What was that?" I gasped with surprise. "Yikes! For goodness sake, woman, be more careful."
preposition	comes before a noun or pronoun and introduces information to the reader about where, when, how, or what kind	on, in, above, by, for Prepositions of time (when): in, on, at "... in the afternoon heat." Prepositions of place (where): in, on, under, behind "... working on the inflatable raft ..."

How can you support your student at home?

- Talk to your student about the first person narrative he or she is writing with a partner and the structure of plot in a narrative.
- Talk to your student about how, when, and why to speed up and slow down time in a narrative.
- Read first person narratives and encourage your student to identify the plot structure in a narrative.
- Invite your student to tell you about the use of conjunctions to combine/join clauses, interjections to express sudden emotions, and prepositions to introduce information about when, where, how, or what kind.
- Play online games on IXL to practice using coordinating conjunctions. For example, IXL Learning. Use Coordinating Conjunctions. Accessed on 17 Jan. 2016. https://www.ixl.com/ela/grade-5/use-coordinating-conjunctions
- Play online games on IXL to practice using prepositions. For example, IXL Learning. Prepositions Review. Accessed on 17 Jan. 2016. https://www.ixl.com/ela/grade-5/prepositions-review

Unit 3: Homework

In Lessons 1–5, homework focuses on research reading and finding the function of conjunctions in specific sentences.

In Lessons 6–12, homework focuses using and determining the function of conjunctions, interjections, and prepositions.

Research reading: Your student is expected to independently research the topic by reading topic-related books of his or her choice for approximately 20 minutes **each day** and responding to a prompt of choice in the **front** of his or her independent reading journal. These are usually books your student will bring home from school; however, they may be topic-related books chosen by the student at the public or home library. Prompts for independent reading can be found in the homework materials provided.

Choice reading: If your student would also like to independently read and respond to a book of free choice, he or she may use the **back** of the independent reading journal. Prompts for independent reading can be found in the homework materials provided.

Lesson	Lesson Content	Homework Practice	Due In	Anticipated Date*
1	Students analyze the point of view in a model first person narrative.	1. Research reading and answering prompt 2. For ELL's: Language Dive Practice I: *Even though*	1. Teacher will check independent reading journals strategically. 2. **Lesson 3**	
2	Students work in pairs to plan and draft the beginning of a first person narrative.	1. Research reading and answering prompt	1. Teacher will check independent reading journals strategically.	
3	Students work in pairs to plan and draft the middle of a first person narrative.	1. Conjunctions Practice I 2. For ELL's: Language Dive Practice II: *Even though* 3. Research reading and answering prompt	1. **Lesson 7** 2. **Lesson 4** 3. Teacher will check independent reading journals strategically.	
4	Students work in pairs to plan and draft the end of a first person narrative.	1. Research reading and answering prompt	1. Teacher will check independent reading journals strategically.	
5	Students work independently to plan and draft a new first person perspective narrative for the mid-unit assessment.	1. Research reading and answering prompt	1. Teacher will check independent reading journals strategically.	
6	Students work in pairs to speed up time where nothing relevant to the plot is happening in their partner narratives.	1. Research reading and answering prompt	1. Teacher will check independent reading journals strategically.	
7	Students work in pairs to slow down time by expanding sentences to add concrete words and phrases and sensory details where something important is happening in their partner narratives.	1. Conjunctions Practice II 2. Research reading and answering prompt	1. **Lesson 9** 2. Teacher will check independent reading journals strategically.	

* Teacher note: Please complete the Anticipated Date column according to your schedule.

Lesson	Lesson Content	Homework Practice	Due In	Anticipated Date*
8	Students work in pairs to slow down time by adding dialogue to show characters response where something important is happening in their partner narratives.	1. Prepositions and Interjections I 2. Research reading and answering prompt	1. **Lesson 11** 2. Teacher will check independent reading journals strategically.	
9	Students practice identifying the function of conjunctions, interjections, and prepositions before completing Part I of the end of unit assessment.	1. Prepositions and Interjections II 2. Research reading and answering prompt	1. **Lesson 11** 2. Teacher will check independent reading journals strategically.	
10	Students revise their narrative written independently in the Mid-Unit 3 Assessment for their End of Unit 3 Assessment.	1. Find a book (fiction) at home, in the library, or on the class bookshelf with a cover that you find eye-catching and inspiring. 2. Research reading and answering prompt	1. **Lesson 12** 2. Teacher will check independent reading journals strategically.	
11	Students work in pairs to write the author's note for their Rainforest Adventures ebook, explaining how they have used concrete and sensory language and dialogue from the first person perspective to help the reader more deeply understand the experience.	1. Find a book (fiction) at home, in the library, or on the class bookshelf with a cover that you find eye-catching and inspiring. 2. Research reading and answering prompt	1. **Lesson 12** 2. Teacher will check independent reading journals strategically.	
12	Students work in pairs to create the front cover and contents page of their ebooks.	1. Research reading and answering prompt	1. Teacher will check independent reading journals strategically.	
13	Students work in pairs to compile their narratives into ebooks.	1. Research reading and answering prompt	1. Teacher will check independent reading journals strategically.	

* Teacher note: Please complete the Anticipated Date column according to your schedule.

Independent Reading

Independent Reading Prompts

Directions: Remember to record responses to **research reading in the front** of your independent reading journal and responses to **choice reading in the back.** Try to choose a different prompt each time.

Record any new vocabulary in your vocabulary log. Remember, academic vocabulary is recorded in the front, and domain-specific vocabulary (words about the topic) is recorded in the back. Mark vocabulary found during independent reading with a symbol—an asterisk (*), for example.

Record:

- Date
- Title and author of your reading book
- Pages you have read
- Prompt
- Response

Example:

Date: 04/08/2018

Book Title and Author: *The Most Beautiful Roof in the World* by Kathryn Lasky

Pages Read: 22–27

Prompt: What questions do you have about the rainforest canopy after reading?

Response: What other animals and plants live in the rainforest canopy?

1. **Record two or three facts in your own words about the rainforest or rainforest animals that you found out in your research reading today.**
2. **What questions do you have about the rainforest or rainforest animals after reading?**
3. **What would you like to research further after reading? Why?**
4. **Summarize your research reading today in no more than four sentences.**

5. **How would you describe the setting of the particular part of the text you read?**
   A. Hint: What did you picture in your mind as you were reading it? Why?
   B. Hint: What did it say in the text to make you think that?
6. **What do you think is going to happen next? Why?**
   A. Hint: What has the author written so far to make you think that?
7. **Summarize the pages you just read in no more than four sentences.**
8. **What is the main idea of the part of the text you just read?**
   A. Hint: The main idea is the point the author wants you to understand.
9. **Think about the title of your text. Why do you think the author chose this title?**
   A. Hint: Explain how the title fits the book.
   B. Hint: Start out: "The title of my book is.... The author chose this title because...."
10. **What are two new words you learned in this text? Tell about the words.**
11. **Choose a picture, chart, graph, or diagram from your text. Explain how the information you learned from the image helped you understand the text.**
    A. Hint: First, think about the main idea of what you just read. Then, think about how the picture, chart, graph, or diagram supports the main idea.

Homework: Language Dive Practice I: Even though

Name: ______________________________ **Date:** ______________

1. **Directions:** Sketch the meaning of this sentence from "Bite at Night":

   Even though I was in a lot of pain, I realized that I needed to alleviate their concerns immediately.

2. Describe the meaning of even though in the sentence. Why do we use even though?

   ____

   ____

   ____

   ____

3. Complete the sentences with your own ideas.

   A. Even though I ______________________________________,

   I realized that ______________________________________.

   B. I realized that I ______________________________________,

   even though I ______________________________________.

Homework: Language Dive Practice II: Even though

Name: ______________________________ **Date:** ____________

1. **Directions:** The sentence below is scrambled. Write it in the correct order:

she realized that	Even though Meg was nervous,	the boys weren't nervous at all.

____

____

____

2. In the sentence you wrote, circle the conjunction. Box the three subjects. Underline the three verbs.

3. Now write the sentence in three clauses:

Clause #1 (with subordinating conjunction)	Clause #2	Clause #3

4. Write the sentence again. This time, use a different conjunction that is similar in meaning: *because, when, though*.

____

____

____

5. Join the two sentences using *even though* or *though*.

The color changes.	+	The shape stays the same.	=	

Homework: Conjunctions Practice I

Name: ______________________________ **Date:** ______________

Directions: Underline the conjunction and describe the function of the conjunction in that sentence:

1. She hasn't finished her homework, but it is due this morning.

   ____

   ____

   ____

2. I did my math homework while I was waiting for my brother to finish school.

   ____

   ____

   ____

3. I thought I had finished my writing when my teacher noticed I had left out some important information.

   ____

   ____

   ____

4. I hope to finish on time, so I should make it home for dinner.

   ____

   ____

   ____

5. I have an umbrella because it is raining.

   ____

   ____

   ____

Homework: Conjunctions Practice II

Name: ______________________________ **Date:** ____________

Directions: Find two conjunctions in your research reading. Record the sentence, underline the conjunction, and explain the function of the conjunction in that particular sentence:

1. Sentence:

____

____

____

Function:

____

____

____

2. Sentence:

____

____

____

Function:

____

____

____

Homework: Interjections and Prepositions Practice I

Name: ______________________________ **Date:** ______________

Directions: Underline the interjections and circle the prepositions in each sentence. Describe the function of the interjection and/or preposition in that sentence:

1. "Yuck! This is disgusting!" she said as she pushed the plate of food away.

   ____

   ____

   ____

2. "Ouch! That hurt!" he hollered after sitting on a prickly wire brush that someone had left on his chair.

   ____

   ____

   ____

3. "Oh no! I forgot to do my homework," she said while they were walking to school.

   ____

   ____

   ____

4. "Wow! This is so amazing!" he said while looking at her artwork.

   ____

   ____

   ____

5. "Yum! This cake is delicious!" she thought as she ate another large piece from her spoon.

   ____

   ____

   ____

Homework: Interjections and Prepositions Practice II

Name: ______________________________ **Date:** ______________

Directions: Find two interjections and two prepositional words or phrases in your research reading. Record the sentence, underline the interjections, circle the prepositions and explain the function of the interjection and/or preposition in that particular sentence. You can choose sentences that have both interjections and prepositions, or you can choose a different sentence for each.

1. Sentence:

   ____

   ____

   ____

   Function:

   ____

   ____

   ____

2. Sentence:

   ____

   ____

   ____

   Function:

   ____

   ____

   ____

3. Sentence:

____

____

____

Function:

____

____

____

4. Sentence:

____

____

____

Function:

____

____

____

Grade 5 Vocabulary Log

Word and Pronunciation What is the word and how do you say it?	**Definition** What does it mean in your own words?	**Translation** What is the translation in your home language?	**Sketch/ Diagram/ Icon**

Grade 5 Vocabulary Log

Word and Pronunciation What is the word and how do you say it?	**Definition** What does it mean in your own words?	**Translation** What is the translation in your home language?	**Sketch/ Diagram/ Icon**

Grade 5 Vocabulary Log

Word and Pronunciation What is the word and how do you say it?	**Definition** What does it mean in your own words?	**Translation** What is the translation in your home language?	**Sketch/ Diagram/ Icon**

Acknowledgments

Project management support, production design, and copyediting services provided by ScribeConcepts.com

Notes

Notes

Notes

Notes

Notes

Notes

Notes